A LOGIC FOR STRATEGY

A LOGIC FOR STRATEGY

DANIEL R. GILBERT, JR.
EDWIN HARTMAN
JOHN J. MAURIEL
R. EDWARD FREEMAN

BALLINGER PUBLISHING COMPANY
Cambridge, Massachusetts
A Subsidiary of Harper & Row, Publishers, Inc.

International Standard Book Numbers:0–88730–205–X (CL)
0–88730–222–X (PB)

Library of Congress Catalog Card Number: 88–11972

Printed in the United States of America

Library of Congress Cataloging-in-Publication Data

A logic for strategy / Daniel R. Gilbert, Jr. . . . [et al.].
    p.   cm.
    Includes bibliographies and index.
    ISBN 0–88730–205–X.   0–88730–222–X (pbk.)
    1. Management—Decision making.   2. Strategic planning.
    I. Gilbert, Daniel R., 1952–   .
    HD30.23.L64   1988
    658.4'012—dc19   88–11972
                                                                                                CIP

To Peggy S. and Kenneth H. Finch
To the Memory of Bill Macomber
To Kenneth R. Andrews
To John Lubin

CONTENTS

LIST OF FIGURES

PREFACE

When is the last time that you sat down and had a conversation with your colleagues, or with yourself, about what *the concept of strategy* means to you? When is the last time you considered *why* you approach strategy in the way that you do, rather than *how*? If it has been too long, we have some ideas that might prove useful for you. We have written this book for the quiet moments in your days when you can read, think, and talk about the very concept of strategy.

This is definitely not an instruction manual about how to do strategy. There are no surefire techniques here for solving thorny strategy problems. If your telephone rings incessantly with calls from customers who feel overcharged and underloved, we have no magic soothing words to offer. If your primary competitor just established a beachhead in your firm's most vulnerable market segment, we have no ready battle plans. If a major shareholder is contacting the rest of your shareholders with more than holiday greeting cards, do not look here for a poison pill remedy. If an investigative reporter or union official has been waiting in your outer office all morning, wanting to see you about a suspected product defect, we can offer no suggestions for defusing the issue. If these are your problems, you need answers to questions about *how* to proceed and *when* to act, or not act, and *how often* to do so. Many writers and consultants stand ready to answer these questions for you. We are not among them.

We deal here with a different kind of question, one that both precedes and permeates the techniques of strategy. We believe that something is lost if a person interested in strategy does not pause and ponder, *"Why do I approach strategy as I do?"*. No coherent answer to this question can be given in the guise of some technique; rather, the question must be answered with a coherent line of reasoning.

We call such reasoning *a logic for strategy*. We hope that you will think about a logic for the concept of strategy and, in the course of conversation with others, will understand your logic for strategy. Only then, we believe, can you understand the contexts in which strategy techniques can and cannot work. In short, we have written a book inviting you to think about the *meaning of strategy*.

The importance of engaging in conversations about strategy—or any management concept, for that matter—cannot be overstated. We have come to see this on two levels. First, we have observed precious little conversation about the meaning of strategy. Inside corporations, the hustle and bustle of daily routines can obscure the need—and consume the time and energy required—for talking about the meaning of those routines. In the popular business press, the emphasis is clearly on selling the latest cure for corporate ills, not on understanding the roots of those ills. In the academic literature, there is virtually no recognition of the value, much less the means, of probing the meaning of strategy. In that arena, many writers implicitly assume that questions of meaning have already been settled.

Secondly, this book has come to fruition in the course of years of conversation among the four of us. Beginning with exchanges between Ed Freeman and Ed Hartman at the University of Pennsylvania, moving to conversations between Ed Freeman and John Mauriel at the University of Minnesota, and then later to hours of debate that eventually included Dan Gilbert at Minnesota, this project is one small testimonial to the benefit of taking a long, critical look at a concept. With time and willingness, you and your colleagues can similarly gain in your understanding of strategy.

It is for this second reason that we want to acknowledge those persons who have helped bring our conversations to these pages, to those persons who have tried to teach us about strategy, and to those persons who have tried to teach us about the value and the pleasure of talking about why we do what we do. We are indebted to them all.

Karen Dickinson at the Colgate Darden Graduate School of Business Administration, University of Virginia, transformed this project from a jumble of cut-and-paste scribblings into a finished manuscript. S. Ven-kataraman at the Carlson School of Management, University of Minnesota, contributed substantially to the research in Chapter 7 about strategic planning processes. Through an independent study project at Bucknell University, Erin McGrath assisted us by gathering materials for the case studies in Chapter 2 and by enduring earlier versions of the manuscript. Ann and Allan Grundstrom provided a quiet retreat replete with a wood stove, firewood, running trails, and vistas on the mountains of central Pennsylvania. Without the patience of Marjorie Richman at Ballinger, our conversations could not have made it to the printed page.

Our strategy teachers deserve both a note of gratitude and perhaps a certain amount of blame for what appears in this book. Ed Freeman thanks Peter Lorange and James Emshoff and extends his dedication to John Lubin. John Mauriel gives special credit to Kenneth R. Andrews. Ed Hartman gives his dedication to the memory of Bill Macomber.

Dan Gilbert has the pleasure of sharing this space with many who have influenced his thinking about strategy. Carol Jacobson's insights about a logic, and certain notable absences of it, for the concept of strategy were influential at a number of points in this project. So, too, were countless conversations with Balaji Chakravarthy at Minnesota; Donald Herman, Daniel McCarthy, John Tomlinson, Lewis Van Antwerp, Robert Courtney, and Elton White at NCR Corporation; Sam Banks at Dickinson College; John Miller and Gordon Meyer at Bucknell University; and John McKeown and Stuart Weiner at Moravian College.

Sharalyn Orbaugh has been a source of inspiration, perspective, and support throughout this project.

As an expression of gratitude for their friendship, Dan makes his dedication to Peggy and Kenneth Finch of New Canaan, Connecticut.

1 IN SEARCH OF A LOGIC FOR STRATEGY

This book is about the concept of strategy. If the concept is new to you, consider this book to be a primer about strategy. If the concept is already familiar to you, but you seek one reasonably condensed and comprehensive survey, then we have something to offer you. This book is also about the state of the art in strategy. This book, still further, is about how well a set of contemporary strategy frameworks deals with the concept of strategy.[1] We provide a reasoned critique, in other words. We have written the book as an invitation for self-reflection about what one has done and/or can do with the concept of strategy.[2]

THE PRINCIPAL PROBLEM

The concept of strategy has reached a crossroads. On one hand, the concept of strategy has become a dominant metaphor for understanding and managing today's corporations. From the global giants like Exxon, IBM, and ITT to the high-tech glamour growth companies like Microsoft and Genentech, we are accustomed to attributing the records of successful corporations to the adoption of a *strategy*. Most executives know what they mean when they say, "We decided to take that action because of our strategy."

1

On the other hand, a growing backlash against strategy is evident among executives and researchers alike. Indeed, some have gone so far as to discard the concept of strategy from their tool kits altogether. Strategy is at a crossroads in two central respects.

First, *the very usefulness of the concept of strategy has come under attack.* Skeptics about strategy abound. In the popular literature, one author after another suggests the death of strategy in some fashion. Some argue that managers' reliance on the concept of strategy is responsible for the decline of American business in the global economy. Others have minted new ideas to replace strategy once and for all. They recommend: forget about strategy and become excellent. They recommend: forget about strategy and become entrepreneurs or intrapreneurs. The substitutes for strategy are numerous: Pay more attention to socialization and collective values. Follow the megatrends. Become one-minute managers (or fifty-nine-second employees). The skeptics urge the adoption of Japanese management techniques and philosophies such as Theory Z and Kanban. They advocate industrial policy. They promote an understanding of the symbolic nature of managerial activities. The list of recommendations is endless, and there is consensus on only one point: pay less attention to strategy.[3]

Scholarly critics are no kinder. Many consider it an illusion to think that chief executives in large corporations are so much in command of their organizations that they can move them in certain directions as troops into battle. They point also to the environment's influence on the organization's fate, against which, they claim, planners' efforts are largely futile.[4] These critics study the relationship between acts of planning and measures of corporate performance and conclude from their ambiguous data that strategy is an anachronism. In distancing themselves from strategy, these critics move to embrace ideas like ecological perspectives or corporate culture management or transaction costs or implementation processes. As with the popular critics, the message is clear: pay less attention to strategy.[5]

Second, *the profusion of strategy models has become a source of confusion for executives and researchers, while many in the research community seem disinterested in finding remedies for this problem.*

Whether familiar with strategy or not, managers may feel overwhelmed by the lengthy succession of new "technologies," each proclaimed as the latest strategic gospel. Complicated analyses explain why, when a new gold mine is discovered in Zaire, uranium holdings in Canada must be sold for strategic reasons. The business press is full of detailed, and inconsistent, explanations of the strategy behind the latest corporate acquisitions. Professors from leading business schools offer seminars in which they will proclaim the finally-discovered, true meaning of strategy—and each has his or her own different version of the truth.

This pattern prompts us to make two observations. First, it is not self-evident how, when, and why the many contemporary models of strategy can and should be applied. Nor is it evident that many researchers care about this state of affairs. Strategy models proliferate. Their proponents devote scant attention, however, to justifying these new interpretations of strategy.[6] To bewildered executives and scholars alike, these authors appear to be saying: "if I can muster the data and tell a different story about strategy, then it is your problem to figure out how to reconcile my story with everything else that you do."

Second, it is not self-evident how to determine if a particular strategy model is *worth* applying. Once again, it is not evident that many researchers care about this point either. An operating corollary to the rule noted above seems to be: "one story about strategy is as good as any other." Critiques of the practice and study of strategy are rare. One can read a long string of articles, or listen to many lectures, about strategy before encountering someone who critically assesses the state of knowledge about strategy.[7] However, even the rare critique may be parochial and ahistorical, with little attention paid to (1) the part strategy plays in the larger context of running a business and (2) the relationship between current conceptions of strategy and our historical and everyday understandings of the concept.[8]

Now, it seems sensible that any strategy model should face a test of relevance to management practice. As we will show shortly, this is clearly the context in which the concept of strategy gained prominence in the first place, dating at least to the ancient Greeks. With this premise as a guide, we might begin to unpack the confusing array of strategy models.

Yet, many academics strongly resist this test, largely because they choose to believe that (1) scientific rigor of a strategy model and (2) the relevance of a model to management practice are two opposing ends.[9] Curiously, many business school deans seem to believe this as well, as they rush to transform their faculties into scientific communities where researchers can remain comfortably aloof from executives.[10] Thus, although management practice seems to be a sensible standard by which to evaluate strategy models, it remains a curiously controversial standard.

A Punch Line

The punch line here is simple. At a juncture when researchers and executives need more than ever to make sense of the concept of strategy in an ongoing dialogue, many on the academic side of that bargain have insulated themselves from their practicing counterparts. Perhaps this is merely an academic response to the critics; perhaps not. We believe that this impedes a more sophisticated understanding of the concept of strategy. Executives and researchers are poorer as a result.

These two facets of the challenge to strategy are distinct and closely related. For even if the critics are incorrect, the proliferation problem among strategy researchers remains. If executives and researchers currently persuaded about the usefulness of strategy cannot find ways to think more carefully about what they are doing, the ranks of the skeptics and agnostics will surely swell. In both senses then, the concept of strategy is truly at a crossroads.

OUR PURPOSE

The primary purpose of this book is to address the challenge to strategy in a critical way. We will take a long, hard look at the concept of strategy as it has evolved and as it is currently applied. We emphasize the underlying reasons why researchers and executives have used the concept of strategy in different ways.[11]

We will examine the roots of the concept of strategy, as well as its criticisms in order to determine where and why the criticisms have merit. In short, the book contains an assessment of the state of the art in strategy.

We make this assessment in several steps. Specifically, we intend to: (1) describe the major elements for each of six well-known models of strategy; (2) provide a means for assessing these six models and the new models of strategy that will inevitably replace them; and (3) appraise the strengths and weaknesses of each of the six models in the context of several contemporary strategic cases. These cases include: (1) the drama surrounding MCI's Execunet long-distance telephone service; (2) the Texaco-Pennzoil standoff; (3) the rise and fall of the Allegis strategy; and (4) the "Twenty-Fifth Man" controversy in Major League baseball. We link all these elements with an idea we call *a logic for strategy*.

OUR ARGUMENT ABOUT A LOGIC
FOR STRATEGY

Our argument is based upon a straightforward premise: the concept of strategy is the most important concept an executive needs for understanding and contributing to the success of a business.[12] To claim that strategy is indispensable is not, however, to show that modern versions of the concept are adequate for the task. Questions about such adequacy have prompted some to suggest that the very concept is not very useful. *Our basic argument is precisely that there is nothing logically wrong with the concept of strategy.*

We will not, however, attempt to defend the concept of strategy by articulating yet another model.[13] Rather, we will show that a return to certain basic ideas about strategy is sorely needed. We will identify several such ideas and argue that, taken together, these ideas constitute *a logic for strategy* upon which strategy's central role in business performance can be justified.[14] Think of a logic as simply a line of argument that is shaped around several basic ideas or principles. Thinking in these terms, you can see that there is a logic to your business, a logic to your own ambitions, a logic to government, and so on.

Why Talk about a Logic for Strategy?

The importance of a logic for the concept of strategy—or any management concept, for that matter—cannot be overstated. We believe that what is missing from the practice and study of strategy is a self-conscious attempt among executives and researchers to justify their efforts.[15] A logic for strategy provides a basis for such reflection in three important respects.

First, without explicit understandings of the ideas upon which various models, or frameworks, of strategy are conceived, executives and researchers alike are helpless in the face of their critics. Second, without such understandings, they are also helpless in the face of their own self-questioning about how they use strategy. Third, without such understandings of their own efforts, strategy researchers cannot respond to the concerns of those who, while persuaded by strategy in general, are confused about the myriad of contemporary strategy models. We will show how a logic for strategy is a powerful tool for understanding how, where, and why the concept of strategy is useful.

A Time-Tested Logic for Strategy

We construct our argument around a logic for strategy consisting of these three principles:

1. *A Principle About Persons.* Whatever else it addresses, a strategy framework must provide for the intentional actions of persons who devise and act on a strategy.
2. *A Principle of Business Basics.* Whatever else it addresses, a strategy framework must pay attention to product quality, customer service, employee commitment, competition, and other fundamental factors.
3. *A Principle of Timely Action.* Whatever else it addresses, a strategy framework must allow management to make timely decisions and to act decisively.

We will elaborate upon each of these principles later in the chapter, but for now suffice it to say that the support for this logic for strategy is quite varied and compelling.[16] The three principles have roots in our historical and everyday understandings of the meaning of "strategy." The logic also is plainly evident in the writings of several early strategy scholars, whose ideas are widely cited by strategy proponents and critics alike. This logic, moreover, reflects a great deal of what the critics of strategy are saying! In short, this logic for strategy is built around some familiar and time-tested ideas.

The growing confusion about strategy can be directly linked to a gap—in places, a chasm—between the logic for strategy that we identify and the central ideas implicit in the array of strategy models in use today. Remember this one key point: divergence from any logic for strategy is something that executives and researchers create, and it is something that they can remedy.[17] But, they must first understand what a logic for strategy is all about. To this matter, we now turn.

THE ROOTS OF A LOGIC FOR STRATEGY

Strategy is an old idea. The word "strategy" comes from the Greek *strategeia*, which means the art or science of being a general (*strategos*). When the Greeks wrote the job description for a general, they most likely stressed three important characteristics.[18]

First, they surely sought a man who could think in terms of acting decisively. The aim was clearly to have someone chart a course of action which held the promise of advantages for those who acted on that plan. That someone was, of course, the general. The Greeks knew well that battles were won or lost because generals did well or badly in deploying the resources of the army. This could mean being clever on the battlefield, or paying attention to supply lines, or thoroughly understanding the terrain, or taking advantage of unexpected opportunities. It could also mean choosing to hide inside a large wooden horse. Regardless of the specific plans he charted, the general clearly dealt in the business of taking intentional actions of an important nature. Our everyday usage of the word "strategic" reflects this: we do not commonly refer to our choices of breakfast cereals and automobile styles as "strategic" matters.

Second, the Greeks surely sought a man who understood that he was not acting in isolation. The successful candidate had to understand that he always needed to take notice of the strategic deliberations of others. Most basic of these other decisionmakers were his troops, his constituents, and his enemies. Our everyday usage of the word "strategic" reflects this same understanding that our actions are part of a larger picture.

The Greeks knew that generals had to attend to certain basic matters. Good generals know how to motivate troops in battle, before, and after. They know how to negotiate with those in authority for supplies and resources, as well as with the enemy for favorable terms of peace. They understand the political as well as the physical environment. They can accurately assess their own strengths and weaknesses, as well as those of the enemy, and deploy infantry and artillery accordingly—or, in some circumstances, not at all. They know the value of alliances. From this point of view, it seems no accident that the diplomat Eisenhower, rather than the battlefield genius Patton, was Supreme Commander in Europe.

Third, the Greeks surely sought for generals those men who could decisively produce plans that contributed to taking timely action. The Greeks sought a general predisposed to action in the first place. Furthermore, the valuable general was one who also had a sense of *when* to act. In order to take timely action, the general had to be willing to leave the drawing board sooner or later.

Strategy's need for timely action is also part and parcel of our common understanding of the concept. Strategy clearly relies on a predisposition to act and a sense of when to act. In order to produce advantages, the general or the executive must know how to fight. But, he must also know how to avoid a fight, especially when he would probably lose. History looks favorably on the valorous riders of the Light Brigade, but not on the generalship of Cardigan, who sent them against superior numbers fortified on high ground. Some senior managers still hold to Cardigan's idea of strategy. (Strategists of this kind may now also take Richard III as a model. His cry has been updated to "My kingdom for a golden parachute!")

The concept of strategy cannot only be traced to the Greeks' military and diplomatic enterprises, but several common threads also link our everyday understanding of strategy with an understanding that can be attributed to the Greeks. The Greeks have left us with an idea that has stood the test of time, time and again.

The Durability of Strategy

Strategy is a durable idea, as a whirlwind scan of human history shows. For as long as humans have struggled to survive in a hostile world and make sense of what William James called its "blooming, buzzing confusion," they have purposefully planned to acquire advantages for themselves. Strategic methods have differed, of course.

Ancient hunters did not gather in boardrooms where they could watch slick presentations with 35mm slides diagramming optimal attack patterns on the mammoth herd. Still, we can picture a small group of prehistoric men discussing how to surround the weakest member of the herd and drive it to a place where it could be killed easily. We can picture these men communicating about their customers who would consume the unfortunate mammoth. We can picture them worrying about the group of hunters who, lurking behind the next glacier, had their sights set on the same herd. While we can imagine that such strategic skills eventually became routine, new challenges inevitably called for new plans. When a particular strategy did not work, the results were clearly measurable and performance reviews were both immediate and not subject to appeal. In that event, the survivors returned to the cave wall drawing board and began their strategic deliberations anew.

Centuries after prehistoric men hunted and the Greeks first spoke and wrote about generalship, yet still long before the Industrial Revolution, sophisticated economic behavior—much of it recognizably strategic—was underway.[19] Farmers, bakers, and craftsmen brought their products to the medieval marketplaces to trade. Like the Greek generals, these people tried to make sense of not only their own intentions about product, price, and marketing techniques, but also the likely actions of others.

By the fifteenth century, the marketplace gave way to more nearly permanent shops and stores, some of which had regular suppliers. Soon the problems of dealing with suppliers and distribution channels became as important for some businessmen as did their competitors' plans. Still, these medieval executives were faced with the same set of strategic concerns that their forebears confronted: "From whom shall I buy, and on what terms? To whom can I sell, and how much, and at what price? Who are my possible competitors? How can I keep the town council from interfering with my business? What might happen to make my business better, or more difficult? What am I trying to do with this business?" These are crucial strategic questions, as important in the fifteenth century as they are for IBM today. To be sure, not all medieval merchants asked themselves these questions, but neither do all their twentieth century counterparts.

The art or science of generalship was catapulted to new heights in the Industrial Revolution. Entrepreneurs seized the day by choosing to adapt technological innovations to their ambitious business plans, thus placing a premium on specialization and coordination in their factories.[20] Through intricate factory management techniques foreign to his prehistoric brethren, the general Henry Ford was able to chart a blueprint for producing black cars that sold profitably at $600 each, while paying his employees handsomely for their efforts.[21]

Still, Ford's approach to strategy did not insure a lasting dominance in the automobile industry. Others like Alfred Sloan charted new courses by taking account of how their plans meshed, for example, with customer preferences for cars painted any color but black and for cars styled in different ways.[22] We can understand business success for pioneers in this era in precisely the same way that we can understand the strategic deliberations of the mammoth hunters, Greek generals, medieval butchers and candlestick makers, and eighteenth century fur trappers in Minnesota's North Woods: we can picture each looking at his own intentional efforts, asking questions like "What am I doing and why am I doing it?" We can understand each taking note that his competitors, customers, and later in time, employees were deliberating in a similar strategic fashion. And, we can imagine each planning and executing timely moves and countermoves in response to the actions of those with whom he, for better or worse, interacted. The concept of strategy is sufficiently durable to span prehistoric safaris, Greek generalship, medieval bartering, and the modern automobile business.

The Concept of Strategy in the Twentieth Century

Strategy may be an old and durable idea, yet interest in the concept per se is a recent phenomenon in the business world.[23] Only within the past half century have executives and researchers dealt explicitly with the notion of strategy. In this era, a widely accepted concept of "strategy" has emerged: *a strategy is a set of important decisions derived from a systematic decisionmaking process conducted at the highest levels of an organization.*[24] As the output from this process, a strategy says something about those present actions that executives believe will, to some degree, affect the corporation's future in some desired way.

The basic idea here is simple and, by now, familiar. The concept of strategy, in both the contemporary and ancient senses, is all about acts of choice. Strategy applies in a world where high-salaried executives and ancient generals alike can believe that, to some degree, the future is theirs to shape through reasoned preparation. In the twentieth century, this basic idea has been recast in terms of a decisionmaking process of utmost importance to senior executives. That process became known first as business policy and later as strategic management.[25]

Our modern conceptions of strategy and strategic management owe a great deal to the efforts of two students of strategy: a telephone company executive named Chester Barnard and a business historian named Alfred Chandler.[26] Barnard and Chandler were both centrally concerned with management practice. Barnard drew on his professional experiences in an attempt to generalize about management practice. Chandler observed certain patterns of organizational designs and asked whether management practices had anything to do with the patterns. Although their approaches differed, both Barnard and Chandler built their arguments around themes that have much in common with the three principles that we will develop in this book. Thus, the arguments by Barnard and Chandler add support for our claim that the contemporary concept of strategy has much in common with strategy in the Greek city-states, prehistoric hunting grounds, medieval marketplaces, and the automobile industry.

Barnard and Chandler on Strategy

Barnard and Chandler, working separately, suggested the same basic proposition: *a strategy matters in a significant way for a corporation.* To Barnard, an executive's attention to questions of intended corporate purpose was an integral component of what he termed "the functions of the executive."[27] Unless they were able to articulate a clear purpose for an organization, Barnard argued, executives could not effectively deal with issues of employee commitment and organizational communication. Without a clear idea of intended direction, in other words, an executive had neither (1) much to offer employees nor (2) much to say to them about the directions their efforts were expected to take.[28]

To Chandler, strategy played a different, but no less central, part in the management of a business. Chandler observed that the shape of corporate decisionmaking structures tended to vary with different kinds of strategies. Chandler, accordingly, is widely associated with the proposition that "structure follows strategy."[29] It was Chandler who specified that thinking strategically involves the twin decisionmaking activities of formulating and then implementing some plan to attain a desired future for the corporation.[30]

The footprints of Barnard and Chandler will be evident throughout the six models of strategy that we introduce later. At the same time, the writings of Barnard and Chandler also reveal an understanding of strategy in terms of persons, "business basics," and timely action.[31] Consider some evidence of their understandings.

Chester Barnard and a Logic for Strategy.   Barnard addressed intentional action in the context of executive decisionmaking. He argued that ". . . a characteristic of the services of executives is that they represent a specialization of the process of making organization decisions—and this is the essence of their functions."[32] That specialization was most prominent, in Barnard's view, regarding matters of purpose and strategic action.[33] Barnard argued that a sense of purpose helped an executive discriminate among the possibilities present in the firm's environment: "As soon as that discrimination takes place, decision is in bud. It is the state of selecting among alternatives."[34]

In recognition of the overriding importance of this process, Barnard asserted, "The individual is always the basic strategic factor in organization."[35] Still, he did not confine intentional action to the executive suite.

To Barnard, an organization was a kind of marketplace, which ". . . consists of the organization's relationships (. . .) with other organizations and with individuals *not* connected with the organization in a cooperative way . . ."[36] Barnard thus provided a broad conception of what we have called "business basics." His framework was sufficiently general to encompass customers and competitors, suppliers and regulators.

What's more, he was not content with merely observing that others could take intentional actions that affected an executive's decisions.[37] Barnard explicitly argued that an executive's decisions had to take account of what others might do in response. Nowhere was this plainer than in his comments about employees' responses to authority.

An executive's authority was meaningless, according to Barnard, unless others accepted it.[38] Recognizing how daring this claim was, Barnard admitted that it might create a "platform of chaos."[39] Still, he maintained that authority can fail ". . . because the individuals in sufficient numbers regard the burden involved in accepting necessary orders as changing the balance of advantage against their interest, and they withdraw or withhold [their] contributions."[40] In short, Barnard warned an executive that he wasn't the only one evaluating the consequences of his decisions. In order to take timely action, an executive needed to consider how and why others might respond, and he needed to prepare responses to others' responses. To Barnard, a "good idea" that failed to win support from others was not much of an idea in the first place.[41] All too many modern executives and researchers fail to understand Barnard's point.

Alfred Chandler and a Logic for Strategy.   Chandler, unlike Barnard, was interested in writing a history of the modern corporation.[42] Yet, like Barnard, he argued that senior executives performed a specialized decisionmaking function that superseded such activities as marketing, production, and finance. Characterizing this function as "the visible hand" that steered the modern corporation, Chandler noted, "While the enterprise may have a life of its own, its present health and future growth surely depend on the individuals who guide its activities."[43]

Chandler drew a distinction between the strategic and day-to-day decisions facing an executive. In the process, he made explicit a point implicit in Barnard's writings—namely, that the art or science of strategy is so crucial and complex that it requires specialized guidance by senior executives. Chandler called these executives "the key men in any enterprise."[44]

While Chandler concentrated on the intentional deliberations of a few "key men" inside a corporation, he argued that the impetus for a strategy began beyond the corporation's walls: "Strategic growth resulted from an awareness of the opportunities and needs—*created by changing population, income, and technology*—to employ existing or expanding resources more profitably.[45] [emphasis added] Chandler emphasized that an executive's basic strategic task was to respond to a host of actions taken by others. He lumped these actions together under the label "market demand."[46] Only when senior executives understood the basic elements of market demand, Chandler argued, were they ready to allocate resources to meet that demand.

Chandler stressed the importance of organization structure as the means for resource allocation and, hence, timely action. In this regard, the executive needed to guide: ". . . the formation of an administrative structure to mobilize systematically the resources within each functional activity . . ."[47]

Because market demand was always evolving, a key test for executives was how quickly they could respond with a structure that supported the firm's strategy in an efficient way. Thus, Chandler described a world in which a firm's strategy and structure were continually evolving because the strategies and structures of other firms—in the form of market demand—were also changing.

In short, Chandler, like Barnard, stressed that timely action began, but did not end, with the initiatives at any one firm. Timely action, they argued, was more complicated than that.

Strategy is a very old idea, yet, it is an evolving one, adapted by observers such as Barnard and Chandler to the problems of the complex modern corporation. We have moved from the ancient hunters and Greek generals to their modern corporate counterparts in order to make one central point: the logic for strategy that we introduced earlier is based on three themes that persist throughout the evolution of the concept of strategy. These themes also shed light on what the critics of strategy are saying.

Three Criticisms of Strategy

In one way or another, the critics of strategy question the very relevance of the concept. We believe that these criticisms reflect a pattern quite similar to the themes that we have been developing throughout this chapter. Specifically, we interpret the critics to be making an argument like this: the modern concept of strategy is less and less relevant because it is tends to *ignore* themes such as those embodied in the Principle about Persons, Principle of Business Basics, and Principle of Timely Action.[48] Let's sharpen this insight by briefly considering three common criticisms of strategy.

"Strategy Ignores Creativity."   The modern application of strategy, some critics argue, has become an institution within many business firms. These

critics paint a very accurate picture of the complex quantitative decision models, never-ending planning "cycles," and elegant presentation techniques that have become synonymous with strategy.[49]

All this, they argue, can easily obscure attention to nurturing the individual creative efforts that must be the lifeblood of any enduring business. These critics are dismayed to find that the heroes of modern strategy look more like "numbers men" such as Harold Geneen, George Steinbrenner, and Robert McNamara, than such creative figures as Steve Wozniak, Bill Gates, Donald Burr, Charley Finley, and Bill Veeck.[50]

The critics deserve to be heard in this regard. Their point is that strategy has spawned so much technical analysis that planning gets in the way of doing anything new.[51] The point has merit. Analytical methods based on internal rates of return, market shares, and discounted cash flow analysis, for example, are inherently biased toward the present. In practice, they function as new and clever means by which staff analysts can say "no" to anyone eager to experiment with an idea. These methods are also biased toward aggregate concepts. What can easily be lost in this emphasis on "hard" analysis is a place for the conscientious actions of living, breathing persons.[52]

These critics seem to suggest that "strategy by the plan" has diverted attention from the parts played by curious persons who exercise judgment and seek creative solutions to new problems. In the sterile world of "strategy by the plan," a senior executive need not ask, "Why are we pursuing this market?" All she has to do is look at the numbers. The product engineer need not ask, "What if we combined this gadget with that widget?" All he has to do is refer to the strategic plan. The account representative need not ask, "What do our customers think about our service?" *What is missing here, the critics might say, is an appreciation for something like our Principles about Persons.*

"Strategy Ignores Product Quality and Customer Service."   Other critics argue that modern models of strategy bear little relation to what is involved in running a business.[53] By relying on certain analytical techniques of strategic planning, such as capital budgeting, cash flow analysis, market share analysis, and internal rates of return, managers have neglected what is most important. The critics claim that these analyses may not have anything to do with a basic business maxim: deliver a quality product in such a manner that customers and employees both gain in the bargain.

The critics deserve to be heard here, too. Tom Peters and Nancy Austin, for example, tell story after story about companies that "smell of customers."[54] By contrast, public pronouncements by airline executives are often laced with terms like "yield management" and strategic "load factors," statistics that can be boosted by assigning more and more airplanes to already crowded airports.[55] What is the effect of larger and larger load factors on customer service? Take a flight these days and see our point.

Other critics note that it has taken years for executives at the American automobile companies to realize that product quality is not an optional investment.[56] Yet, the latest heroes in strategic management are those executives who have mastered the art of corporate restructuring. This art often goes by a more familiar label: cost cutting.[57] Only rarely is restructuring defended as a means to product quality improvement.

Finally, it is not self-evident that strategic restructuring analyses routinely account for the effects on individual employees. As both example and metaphor, the midnight move of the Baltimore-now-Indianapolis Colts football franchise says a great deal about the connection between strategy and persons in the 1980s.[58]

In sum, *some of the criticisms of strategy point to how far strategy has strayed from something like our Principle of Business Basics.*

"Strategy Invites Paralysis."   Still other critics of strategy are dismayed by such statements as, "We had a great strategy, but no one would implement it." To these critics, any management concept that does not provide a blueprint for timely action is simply incoherent. Imagine a civil engineer complaining, "We designed a perfect bridge, but the law of gravity got in the way." Imagine an urban planner observing, "We had a beautiful design for the downtown mall, but politics got in the way." Modern strategy models, some critics claim, rely on precisely such reasoning. Think of how often you hear or read an explanation like, "We had a great strategy, but our _____ interfered." Fill in the blank with "competitors" or "employees" and you see the point. There is something about strategy, the critics say, that sidesteps timely action.

These critics deserve to be heard as well. They call our attention to the assumptions strategic planners make about human nature. If planners presume that managers and employees will automatically adopt any new strategic plan that has the "right numbers," it is no wonder then that "implementation problems" emerge.[59] This also holds true if strategic planners assume that competitors will sit tight. Such an assumption clearly downplays the diversity among persons in and around a corporation. Consequently, strategic action can become paralyzed.

As a general concept of human nature, the assumption that resistance to a strategy can be wished away is simply false. Everyone connected with an organization has his or her own agenda. Why are they connected with the organization in the first place? Strategic plans sometimes fit with these agendas; sometimes, not. To suppose that this will all change when "the plan says so" is an exercise in self-delusion.

This line of criticism suggests that strategic planning can readily miss the point of our Principle of Timely Action. Unless strategy models are based on assumptions that realistically account for the difficulties in executing a strategy, managerial action can quickly become an exercise in paralysis.

In sum, the varied criticisms of strategy have some important things in common with the themes upon which our logic for strategy is built. We devote the rest of the book to assessing the strength of the critics' case. Let's conclude the chapter by revisiting the three principles that constitute our version of a logic for strategy.

THREE PRINCIPLES

A Principle about Persons emphasizes that, for better or worse, strategy turns on the intentional actions taken by a host of persons:

> Whatever else it addresses, a strategy framework must provide for the intentional actions of persons who devise and act on a strategy.

Intentional action certainly does not imply that persons achieve or know everything that they seek. Nor does it imply that strategy is something that one does alone. We almost hesitate to make such an obvious assertion, except that it is not universally accepted among students of strategy.[60]

We identify this principle first for a simple reason. We believe that the most important factor in strategy is the part that persons play in the shaping and execution—for better or worse—of strategy. Put differently, the study and practice of strategy is pointless if no allowance is made for the intentional actions of human beings. We will show that each strategy framework is predicated upon certain assumptions about persons and intentional action. The measure of compliance then with our Principle about Persons is the complexity with which persons are portrayed in a given framework.

A Principle of Business Basics calls attention to the intersection of various actions taken in the name of strategy:

> Whatever else it addresses, a strategy framework must pay attention to product quality, customer service, employee commitment, competition, and other fundamental factors.

This principle holds that talking about intentional actions taken in the name of strategy is pointless if the actions of customers, employees, and competitors are indistinct or missing. The measure of compliance with this principle rests with: (1) the range of human beings identified as having a part to play with regard to a strategy; and (2) the distinctiveness with which those persons are portrayed. In short, our Principle of Business Basics calls attention to particular persons introduced through our Principle about Persons.

Finally, a Principle of Timely Action stresses the immediacy with which strategic action can and should be taken:

> Whatever else it addresses, a strategy framework must allow management to make timely decisions and to act decisively.

This principle holds that, given the importance of strategy, a framework must provide a blueprint for action with those players identified in the Principle of Business Basics. Put somewhat differently, this principle stresses both the immediacy and the enduring nature of any strategic relationship. If a strategy framework cannot guide us to answer the question, "What do we do now that _____ has acted?", it fails to account for enduring situations. For any given strategy framework, the measure of compliance with this principle rests with the attention given to when action should or should not be taken.

The Plan for This Book

Many stories have been told about strategy. The six stories that we will examine are well-known variations on the same theme: a strategy is a set of important decisions for the firm. The six stories also represent a varied lot. By showing that each can be analyzed in terms of our logic for strategy, we will show that the concept of strategy is indeed relevant and durable.

For each strategy framework, we will conduct our analysis in terms of the three principles introduced above. Moreover, we will apply these principles to a given framework in the context of some complex contemporary strategic problems. These problems, briefly narrated in Chapter 2, include strategic events at MCI and AT&T, Texaco and Pennzoil, Allegis, and Major League baseball.

In Chapter 3, we examine what we call the Harvard Policy framework, so-called because this concept of strategy originated in teaching and research that began at the Harvard Business School and, in particular, in the Business Policy course in Harvard's MBA curriculum. The main idea here is that strategy should be understood as the pattern of purposes and policies that define the company and its businesses.

We then move in Chapter 4 to the Portfolio framework, so-called because its proponents borrow some ideas from portfolio theory in finance. The main principle here is that a diversified company is like a portfolio of stocks. Just as investors seek an optimal investment strategy for their securities, managers should seek a strategy that maximizes return on a group of businesses that make up a corporation.

The Competitive Strategy framework, the subject of Chapter 5, is based on the notion that strategy is a matter of (1) discerning the economic forces (mostly macro-economic) that shape industrial performance and (2) aligning the business with those forces to achieve success.

A fourth model of strategy is the Stakeholder Management framework, addressed in Chapter 6. This model focuses on how executives can manage relationships with the individuals and organizations holding long-term stakes in the company's operations.

A fifth strategy model deals directly with the processes of making strategic decisions for a corporation. This Planning Process framework is the subject of Chapter 7, where we discuss several variations on the basic theme that the decisionmaking process is a manager's top priority.

The last model is called the Seven-S Framework, simply because all seven key variables begin with "S": strategy, structure, systems, staff, style, skills, and superordinate goals. The Seven-S Framework is the subject of Chapter 8.

In Chapter 9, we provide a brief comparative assessment of the state of the art in strategy. We will *not* try to put all the frameworks together into a mega-model of strategy. In fact, we will provide some good reasons for not trying to do that at all. We will also suggest where the practice and study of strategy can and should go from here.

A NOTE TO OUR READERS

The explanation and evaluation of these strategy frameworks is intended to benefit a variety of readers. Of particular interest to us are managers and academics. If you are a practicing manager, our advice is to think about your own business as you read each chapter. Think about whether and how each framework can help you understand the logic of your business. If the notes look boring or beside the point, ignore them. We have collected an annotated bibliography at the end of each chapter in order to point you toward more information about the ideas that interest you.

If you are an academic who is teaching and doing research about business, the most interesting aspect of the book for you may be the critical commentary about strategy. We offer some remarks that have not appeared in the existing literature. The extensive notes are written with you in mind. We have simplified complex arguments in the text and then complicated some of them again in the notes. There, too, you will find discussions of the contributions of others to the literature about strategy.

We now invite you to join us in reflecting about a logic for strategy.

NOTES TO CHAPTER 1

1. We are interested here in the interpretations that the members of a community of researchers have given to a concept that they hold in common: namely, strategy. Ours is an introductory study about how and why certain members of this community have chosen to interpret strategy. It is introductory in the sense that we make no attempt to place strategy in some larger social context. At the same time, this kind of analysis has not been attempted—either in scope or critical detail—before in the strategy research literature.

2. The book is not, however, about the state of what might be called the science of strategy. Pick up any issue of *Strategic Management Journal*, for example, and you will see that that enterprise is alive and well. We maintain, however, that science is pointless without an understanding of the reasons for pursuing scientific studies in the first place. We perceive science as simply another form of discourse which, like any human discourse, needs to be justified through critical analysis.

3. Freeman and Gilbert argue that, once we understand the close connection between strategy and ethics, the abandonment of strategy as a standard of

value is an incoherent prescription for management. They argue that the choice is not between strategy and excellence, for example, but between different strategy alternatives that each embody a measure of excellence. See R. Edward Freeman and Daniel R. Gilbert, Jr., *Corporate Strategy and the Search for Ethics* (Englewood Cliffs, N.J.: Prentice-Hall, 1988).

4. For a classic statement of this position, see Gareth Morgan, "Rethinking Corporate Strategy: A Cybernetic Perspective," *Human Relations* 36, no. 4 (1983): 345–60; or anything written about a population ecology approach to organizations.

5. Consider the editorial content of the infant *Academy of Management Executive*, a journal created as a means for academics to talk to executives. Strategy is largely missing from those pages. Where the concept is addressed, it is treated as an optional contributor to organizational performance. For example, see John A. Pearce, III and Fred David, "Corporate Mission Statements: The Bottom Line," *Academy of Management Executive* 1, no. 2 (1987): 109–16. The problem with such research, as we show in Chapter 7, is that its perpetrators confuse *strategy* with the act of *forming* a strategy.

6. Justification is simply a matter of giving reasons to other members of a community who then can decide whether those reasons are coherent or not. For two accounts about why many social scientists resist giving justifications, see Richard Rorty, *Consequences of Pragmatism* (Minneapolis, Minn.: University of Minnesota Press, 1982), pp. 90–109; and Alasdair MacIntyre, *After Virtue*, 2d ed. (Notre Dame, Ind.: University of Notre Dame Press, 1984), pp. 23–35.

7. Criticism, in a formal rather than naive sense, is a matter of asking questions about the meanings of concepts, variables, research findings, and so on. Criticism, as we will show in Chapter 9, involves taking concepts apart and considering their usefulness in certain contexts. Yet, many researchers seem to want to bypass this exercise and simply synthesize whatever concepts they can derive. Criticism is an unnecessary bother on this account. Consider what the incoming chair in the Academy of Management's Business Policy & Planning Division has to say about the state of strategy: "With all of the success we have had there is still far to go. . . . Colleagues in other fields still criticize the conceptual foundations of our field, recently with seemingly renewed stridency." See "Letter from the Incoming Chair," *Business Policy & Planning Division Newsletter* (Academy of Management, Autumn 1987), p. 2. The implication is clearly that criticism in any form is a problem to be eradicated.

8. Put somewhat differently, the concept of strategy is pointless if not connected to some theory of the firm, for which a strategy gives direction. Now, pick up a standard strategy textbook and search for anything about a theory of the firm. You will come up empty-handed. For one example of how to make this connection, see R. Edward Freeman, *Strategic Man-*

agement: A Stakeholder Approach (Boston, Mass.: Pitman, 1984), pp. 1–23.

9. For an argument about how these two concepts cannot be separated, see R. Edward Freeman and Peter Lorange, "Theory Building in Strategic Management," in R. Lamb and P. Shrivastava, eds., *Advances in Strategic Management*, Vol. 3 (Greenwich, Conn.: JAI Press, 1985), pp. 9–38.

10. See, for example, the comments attributable to Raymond Miles at the University of California, Berkeley, in James W. Schotter, "An Interview with Dean Raymond E. Miles," *Selections* (Graduate Management Admission Council, Spring 1987), pp. 13–17. Miles misses the point of dialogue between researcher and executive when he argues that "if we're only involved with issues from a problem-solving perspective, we're not doing anything different from what the managers should be doing. As educators, our role must be different" (p. 13).

11. We have been heavily influenced here by the arguments of Richard Rorty. See, in particular, Richard Rorty, "The Historiography of Philosophy: Four Genres," in R. Rorty, J. Schneewind, and Q. Skinner, eds., *Philosophy in History* (Cambridge: Cambridge University Press, 1984), pp. 49–75.

12. Think of *strategy* as the answer to the question, "What shall I [or we] do in this context?" This book is not a proof that this concept of strategy deserves special status, nor do we appeal to some objective reality where strategy is a fixed point or first principle. We only (!) argue that questions about strategy, or intended future direction, can serve managers well as a means for interpreting their own actions.

13. It is common practice in strategy research to rescue a floundering concept by tethering it to some firmer concept. This synthetic urge is one that we resist for reasons that will be spelled out in Chapter 9. Thus, ours is not some attempt at producing a "meta" theory about strategy.

14. We are interpreters in this enterprise. The data that we examine consists of the arguments made by a set of strategy researchers. For a fuller account of strategy research as interpretation, see Daniel R. Gilbert, Jr. and Carol K. Jacobson, "Stakeholders, Ideology, and Enterprise Strategy" (Paper for Annual Meeting of the Academy of Management, New Orleans, Louisiana, August 1987); and Daniel R. Gilbert, Jr., "Strategy and Justice" (Ph.D. diss., University of Minnesota, 1987), chap. 2.

15. An ongoing discourse on justification amounts to a critical research tradition. Such discourses have emerged, rather noisily, in such professional fields as law and medicine. For a basic overview of these developments, see Jerry Frug, "Henry James, Lee Marvin, and the Law," *New York Times Book Review*, February 16, 1986, pp. 1, 28–29.

Critical management research may not paint a pretty picture. For some glimpses of this, see Freeman and Gilbert *Corporate Strategy*, chap. 7; and Daniel R. Gilbert, Jr. and R. Edward Freeman, "The Flight from

Meaning: A Critical Interpretation of the Management Classics" (Paper for the Critical Perspectives in Organizational Analysis Conference, Baruch College–CUNY, New York, September 1985).

16. This support is replicable, in other words, across a variety of contexts. For a discussion about why replicability is pertinent here, see Robert K. Yin, *Case Study Research: Design and Methods* (Beverly Hills, Calif.: Sage, 1984), chaps. 1, 2.

17. See Rorty, *Consequences of Pragmatism*, regarding science as a kind of writing.

18. We are engaged here in the philosophical enterprise known as rational reconstruction which, as Rorty notes, involves imagining ourselves carrying on a conversation with the Greek generals about some concept held in common. See Rorty, *Philosophy in History*. The value in doing this rests with understanding that our present-day conceptions of strategy can be enriched by understanding the history of strategy. We need not, in other words, reinvent the wheel of strategy, if we so choose.

19. See Fernand Braudel, *The Structures of Everyday Life: Civilization and Capitalism 15th–18th Century*, Vol. 1 (New York, Harper and Row, 1982).

20. Many modern-day researchers want to deny this, arguing instead that technology is some disembodied, metatheoretical force that drives human action. For an argument about the problems with such a perspective, see John Child, "Organizational Structure, Environment, and Performance: The Role of Strategic Choice," *Sociology* 6 (1972): 1–22.

21. See David Halberstam, *The Reckoning* (New York: Avon, 1986) for a very readable history of Ford Motor Company.

22. See Alfred D. Chandler, Jr., *Strategy and Structure* (Cambridge, Mass.: M.I.T. Press, 1962), pp. 114–162; and Alfred P. Sloan, *My Years with General Motors* (New York: Doubleday, 1963), for example.

23. For an insightful early account, see Igor Ansoff, *Corporate Strategy: Business Policy for Growth and Expansion* (New York: McGraw-Hill, 1965).

24. Gilbert, "Strategy and Justice," refers to this as the dominant "strategy through process" genre of strategy research. Discussions with Professor Andrew Van de Ven have helped clarify this point.

25. See Dan E. Schendel and Charles W. Hofer, "Introduction," in D. E. Schendel and C. W. Hofer, eds., *Strategic Management: A New View of Business Policy and Planning* (Boston, Mass.: Little, Brown, 1979), pp. 5–13.

26. The principal sources here are: Chester I. Barnard, *The Functions of the Executive*, 30th Anniversary Edition (Cambridge, Mass.: Harvard University Press, 1968); Alfred D. Chandler, Jr., *Strategy and Structure* (Cambridge, Mass.: M.I.T. Press, 1962), and Alfred D. Chandler, Jr., *The Visible Hand: The Managerial Revolution in American Business* (Cambridge, Mass.: Belknap Press, 1977).

27. See Barnard, *The Functions of the Executive*, pp. 215–34.

28. Ibid., pp. 227–39.

29. For an introduction to this proposition, see Chandler, *Strategy and Structure*, pp. 1–17 and, in particular, p. 13.

30. Ibid., p. 13.

31. As we observed in note 18, we are engaged in rational reconstruction in this part of the analysis. Neither Barnard nor Chandler explicitly used our three principles. But, their arguments could have enabled us to converse with them on these subjects. In this way, we can show you a continuity in how persons have chosen to interpret the concept of strategy.

32. See Barnard, *The Functions of the Executive*, p. 189.

33. Ibid., pp. 196–99, 231–34.

34. Ibid., p. 197.

35. Ibid., p. 139.

36. Ibid., p. 241.

37. Ibid., pp. 240–56.

38. Ibid., pp. 161–84.

39. Ibid., pp. 164–65.

40. Ibid., p. 165.

41. We will show that many researchers have failed to understand, or have chosen to ignore, Barnard in this regard. Prime evidence of this is the widespread belief that strategy formulation and strategy implementation are separate actions.

42. See Chandler, *Strategy and Structure*, pp. 1–7.

43. Ibid., p. 8.

44. Ibid., p. 11.

45. Ibid., p. 15.

46. Ibid., pp. 383–96.

47. Ibid., p. 385.

48. Once again, we are rationally reconstructing a possible dialogue with our counterparts who criticize the concept of strategy.

49. Some analytical techniques—many associated with operations research and finance, for example—contribute to efficient operation without getting at the basics of the business. That such models oversimplify the complexity of running a business is not a negative feature; all good theories and models oversimplify, which is why they must be used with care. Problems arise when their usefulness in a restricted area seduces the user into thinking that the key to the business is a maximization algorithm or computing the optimal hurdle rate for new projects.

50. A principal expression of such dismay runs throughout Thomas J. Peters and Robert H. Waterman, Jr., *In Search of Excellence* (New York: Harper & Row, 1982). If you want to draw your own conclusions about this distinction, read Harold Geneen, with Alan Moscow, *Managing* (New

York: Doubleday, 1984) alongside Bill Veeck and Ed Linn, *Veeck as in Wreck* (Evanston, Ill.: Holtzman Press, 1981).

51. A well-known argument in this regard is given in Robert H. Hayes and William J. Abernathy, "Managing Our Way to Economic Decline," *Harvard Business Review* 58, no. 4 (1980): 67–77. See also Daniel H. Gray, "Uses and Misuses of Strategic Planning," *Harvard Business Review* 64, no. 1 (1986): 89–97; and Robert H. Hayes, "Why Strategic Planning Goes Awry," *New York Times*, April 20, 1986, p. 2F.

52. To get some sense of this, read Henry Mintzberg and James A. Waters, "Of Strategies, Deliberate and Emergent," *Strategic Management Journal* 6 (1985): 257–72, and look for persons and their actions in that narrative.

53. If you want to get some sense of this criticism, but your time is in short supply, look through Richard G. Hamermesh, *Making Strategy Work: How Senior Managers Produce Results* (New York: John Wiley & Sons, 1986) and see whether you can find references to customers. Making "strategy work" independent of customers, the critics argue, is a contradiction.

54. See Tom Peters and Nancy Austin, *A Passion for Excellence* (New York: Random House, 1985); and Bro Uttal, "Companies That Serve You Best," *Fortune*, December 7, 1987, pp. 98–116.

55. See Kenneth Labich, "Winners in the Air Wars," *Fortune*, May 11, 1987, pp. 68–79, and study the language used to describe competition and strategy.

56. See "Can Ford Stay on Top?", *Business Week*, September 28, 1987, pp. 78–86.

57. See Maggie McComas, "Cutting Costs Without Killing the Business," *Fortune*, October 13, 1986, pp. 70–78, and Bill Saporito, "Cutting Costs Without Cutting People," *Fortune*, May 25, 1987, pp. 26–32. A more sobering perspective is presented in Ralph E. Winter, "Trying to Streamline, Some Firms May Hurt Long-Term Prospects," *Wall Street Journal*, January 8, 1987, pp. 1, 10.

58. See Freeman and Gilbert, *Corporate Strategy*, chaps. 7 and 8.

59. Implementation researchers, ironically, often seek to ignore human nature altogether. Gilbert, "Strategy and Justice," chap. 3, has detected this in a variety of passages from Lawrence G. Hrbeniak and William F. Joyce, *Implementing Strategy* (New York: Macmillan, 1984).

60. Pick up any issue of *Strategic Management Journal* and check how often you even find references to managers, much less read about what managers do. We will show in this book that there are some clear reasons for this.

ANNOTATED BIBLIOGRAPHY

If you had a month to start from scratch in your understanding of strategy, here are five books that we recommend:

Allison, Graham T. *Essence of Decision*. Boston, Mass.: Little, Brown, 1971.

Greenberg, Eric Rolfe. *The Celebrant*. New York: Penguin, 1983.

McDonald, John. *The Game of Business*. New York: Anchor Press, 1977.

Schelling, Thomas C. *The Strategy of Conflict*. Cambridge, Mass.: Harvard University Press, 1960.

Schelling, Thomas C. *Micromotives and Macrobehavior*. New York: Norton, 1978.

2 FOUR STORIES ABOUT STRATEGY

A strategy is, in simple terms, a significant choice.[1] The practice of strategy involves making choices about (1) an intended future outcome for some joint effort and (2) the route to that intended outcome.[2] The purpose of this chapter is to introduce you to four contemporary cases about the practice of strategy. We will return to these cases often, beginning in Chapter 3, to illustrate the key elements in each of the six strategy frameworks. Think of these cases, then, as a story line in our analysis of strategy.

Throughout the story line, we encounter managers struggling with complex questions about intended future outcomes:

1. After years of battling the American Telephone and Telegraph Company (AT&T) over the interconnection of the MCI microwave telephone network to the Bell System network, MCI Chief Executive Officer William McGowan must decide in 1974 what to do about MCI's long-distance telephone business. He responds with a controversial service called Execunet.
2. In December 1985, a Texas court judge rules that Texaco owes Pennzoil more than $11 billion in damages and interest for interfering with a short-lived Pennzoil-Getty merger agreement. Pennzoil Chairman Hugh Liedtke must decide how and when to collect on the

award. As Texaco lawyers desperately seek delays from the courts, Liedtke decides to hold out for every last penny.

3. After a contentious labor dispute with pilots at United Airlines and amidst growing challenges to United's position in the domestic airline industry, United Chairman Richard Ferris must decide how to distinguish United from its competitors. In 1985, Ferris launches his plan to develop an integrated travel services company, and renames the company "Allegis."

4. During a 1986 season marked by mediocre performance from the Minnesota Twins baseball team, general manager Andy MacPhail must decide whether to break a tacit agreement with his counterparts at other teams and add a twenty-fifth player to the team's roster. Despite season-long problems with performances by Twins pitchers, MacPhail decides to forgo the extra player.

We will give brief accounts of these cases, using our logic for strategy as the basis for pointing out what these managers are doing. Our logic is simply a guide to the relevant information needed to understand the problems facing McGowan, Liedtke, Ferris, and MacPhail.[3] In each instance, a Principle about Persons calls attention to who is involved. A Principle of Business Basics points to those key issues that require urgent attention according to our Principle of Timely Action. Our analyses in Chapters 3 through 8 address how well each strategy framework channels this relevant information.

THE CASE OF EXECUNET

No one could accuse MCI Chairman William McGowan of avoiding a challenge.[4] McGowan simply wanted to operate a nationwide telephone business in direct competition with AT&T. At first glance, the idea seemed preposterous to many people. After all, AT&T (or the Bell System) had operated as a virtual monopoly in the American telephone industry since before World War I. Moreover, that monopoly had been tacitly—and, on several occasions, explicitly—sanctioned by Federal and state government officials. The dedication of Bell System employees who provided "universal service" to every telephone user in the United States was legendary. Why anyone would want to tamper with the best telephone system in the world was beyond the comprehension of many people, including AT&T executives.

McGowan was one of a few entrepreneurs not impressed with the status quo in the telecommunications industry. While some focused on the manufacture of telephone equipment, McGowan looked to the lucrative long-distance business. For decades, the only way to make a long-distance call in the United States was to use the Bell System. With the tacit approval of Federal and state regulators, AT&T executives subsidized rates for local telephone service with revenues derived from the long-distance business. McGowan, who joined a fledgling MCI in the late 1960s, knew that advances in microwave technology made it possible to offer long-distance service at rates far below those charged by AT&T. His first target was the market for intracompany long-distance communications across so-called private lines.

The MCI plan was straightforward: build a separate microwave network; connect that network to the Bell System; set rates that significantly undercut AT&T prices for business customers, yet still yielded a profit. It took MCI six years to even obtain an operating license from the Federal Communications Commission (FCC). It took three more years to prepare the MCI network for the first transmission in 1972. It took two more years—with aid from the FCC and Federal courts—to overcome AT&T resistance to the interconnection of MCI private lines with the Bell network. By April 1974, MCI finally had arrived, or so it appeared.

In truth, MCI was more vulnerable than ever. McGowan was not alone in the private-line business. In fact, the FCC was actively encouraging the development of private networks to introduce competition to the telecommunications industry. AT&T executives watched these events closely. In the fall of 1973, AT&T Chairman John DeButts publicly denounced FCC "experiments" with competitive inroads into AT&T's monopoly territory. DeButts mounted a vigorous campaign to undercut MCI's private-line prices and even ordered disconnection of MCI lines late in 1973.

DeButts's furious retaliation chilled McGowan's efforts to attract and retain major corporate customers. With his attention diverted to regulatory matters, McGowan had little time to tackle problems with the quality of MCI lines. DeButts's campaign also had a chilling effect on MCI employees, as the uncertainty over MCI's interconnection status triggered major layoffs. More worrisome still for McGowan was a growing restlessness among MCI's lenders. By April 1974, MCI still had not recorded a positive monthly cash flow.

McGowan decided to go for broke and enter the long-distance market for *residential* customers as well as business users with a new service dubbed "Execunet." By pairing private lines with an off-the-shelf control device, MCI engineers readily resolved any technical questions about Execunet. And, by cleverly—deviously, according to some—filing a composite tariff with the FCC, McGowan slipped Execunet past the Commission even though MCI's license forbade entry into the residential market.

Neither DeButts nor FCC Chairman Richard Wiley, a consistent supporter of MCI, was amused. Once again, McGowan found himself in the Federal courts, which upheld MCI's right to market Execunet in November 1976. Wiley and DeButts sought a review by the United States Supreme Court. Meanwhile, Execunet proved to be the winner that McGowan had desperately sought. In October 1976, MCI recorded its first positive monthly cash flow. However, the Execunet saga was far from over.

When the Supreme Court justices declined to review the case in January 1978, DeButts decided once again to refuse any new interconnections of Execunet to the Bell network. The cycle of judicial review was repeated. First, Execunet was upheld in a U.S. District Court. When the Supreme Court justices once again refused to grant Wiley and DeButts their day in court in November 1978, McGowan had finally carved a place for MCI alongside AT&T.

THE DISAPPEARING BILLION-DOLLAR HANDSHAKE

One could hardly blame Pennzoil Chairman Hugh Liedtke for celebrating the arrival of 1984 with added fervor.[5] In the first few days of the new year, Liedtke had forged an agreement in principle with the Getty Oil Board of Directors that would permit Pennzoil to acquire Getty. In buying Pennzoil's way into the oil industry "big leagues," Liedtke had to convince representatives of the Getty family, who controlled more than 50 percent of the Getty stock, to sell. His offer was persuasive, and the deal complex. However, by January 3, 1984, Liedtke had obtained agreements in principle with both the Getty family and the Getty directors.

Still, Liedtke had only what amounted to a handshake from the Getty directors. Less than a week later, that handshake disappeared. Texaco Chairman and CEO John McKinley heard of the Getty board action and quickly entered a more attractive bid. On January 8, the Getty directors and the Getty trustees reneged on the deal with Liedtke. Getty now belonged to Texaco. Liedtke soon filed suit in a Texas court on Pennzoil's behalf. In November 1985, the jury awarded a record judgment of more than $11 billion against Texaco for interfering with the Pennzoil–Getty merger. Not until April 1988 did Liedtke and Pennzoil collect a cent.

Even though they were stunned by the enormity of the judgment, McKinley and his legal advisers initially thought they only had to mount a convincing appeal of the verdict. They soon learned otherwise.

In order to protect claimants such as Pennzoil, Texas law provided that Pennzoil could attach liens on Texaco assets. Moreover, Texaco could be required to post a bond for the entire amount of the court award. McKinley knew that Texaco could not afford to comply with either encumbrance if it hoped to maintain its credit lines. Unless given a reprieve on the encumbrance issue, McKinley was prepared to file for Texaco's bankruptcy. When a temporary reprieve was granted by the state court, McKinley embarked upon an appeals campaign at the state and Federal levels.

Liedtke chose a different route. From the very beginning of the appeals saga, he was willing to wait for McKinley to agree on an out-of-court settlement. Liedtke had to tread carefully here. The possibility of a Texaco bankruptcy clouded the likelihood of Pennzoil's collecting the full amount of the award. Under Chapter 11 protection for Texaco, Pennzoil became one of many unsecured creditors. Still, Liedtke agreed several times over the next sixteen months to defer exercising Pennzoil's rights to attach Texaco assets. Liedtke wanted a deal from Texaco.

Liedtke, McKinley, and, after McKinley's retirement, CEO James Kinnear, and Chairman Alfred DeCrane discussed many possible settlements. Texaco offered to sell Getty to Pennzoil after all. Texaco offered to buy certain of Pennzoil's businesses, but Liedtke was unwilling to trade Pennzoil customers to his fiercest rivals. Texaco offered a straight cash settlement that Liedtke publicly belittled. The Texaco executives even proposed a "friendly" takeover of Pennzoil by Texaco, which Liedtke rejected. One of his reasons for doing so was Texaco's refusal to guarantee retention of Pennzoil employees. In the end, Liedtke found none of the offers satisfactory.

The end came sooner than Liedtke perhaps had expected. Early in April 1987, the U.S. Supreme Court justices stripped Texaco of protection from the Texas lien laws. Kinnear and DeCrane approached Liedtke one more time without success. On April 12, papers were filed to place Texaco under Federal bankruptcy protection. Not only had the original handshake disappeared, but so had the $11 billion payment. Eight months later, as 1987 drew to a close, Kinnear and DeCrane succumbed to pressure from several key Texaco shareholders and agreed to a $3 billion settlement with Pennzoil. Liedtke accepted the deal.

ALL TOGETHER UNDER THE ALLEGIS BANNER

From the outset, UAL Chairman Richard Ferris was not a typical senior airline executive.[6] Trained in hotel and food service management, Ferris joined UAL, parent company for United Airlines, in 1971 and was named CEO in 1979. As he led United through the DC-10 crisis, the newly-deregulated airline marketplace, the air traffic controllers' strike, and a 1982 strike by United pilots, Ferris began to envision UAL as more than just an airline. By the middle of 1985, he was ready to move on his idea.

To be sure, United was not just another airline. Until Texas Air Chairman Frank Lorenzo embarked on his ambitious acquisition program in the mid-1980s, United was the largest domestic passenger carrier. Lorenzo's ambitions, coupled with stiff competitive threats from American, Delta, and Northwest Airlines, prompted Ferris to seek a different way to compete for customers. That different approach proved to be nothing less than a radical redefinition of the businesses that made up UAL. Because revamping was to be complete, Ferris intended to abandon the "UAL" label altogether.

Ferris's strategy was to transform UAL, the airline company, into the new "Allegis," a diversified and integrated travel company. By serving airline passengers from one end of the trip to the other, Ferris hoped to give United a competitive edge in the airline industry. Ferris's knowledge of the hotel business gave the plan all the more impetus.

Ferris moved swiftly and boldly on the plan. Over an eighteen-month period beginning in June 1985, UAL spent an estimated $2.3 billion to acquire a rental-car business (Hertz), a trans-Pacific route system (from Pan American), and a hotel chain (Hilton). In February 1987, Ferris formally announced the "Allegis" name and embarked on a major promotional campaign.

Almost overnight, opposition festered.

In April, United pilots unveiled a plan to buy United Airlines from Allegis. Still embittered by Ferris's stance during the 1982 strike, the pilots argued that Hertz and Hilton siphoned off the cash generated by airline operations. Several major investors agreed. While the pilots were developing their proposal, real estate magnate Donald Trump accumulated a 4.9 percent stake in Allegis. Trump publicly likened the "Allegis" name to the name of a disease.

Trump sold his holdings at the end of April. In May, Ferris had to contend with a new headache. Three principals in an investment firm known as Coniston revealed their 13 percent stake in Allegis. The Coniston partners announced plans to unseat the Allegis board and hinted at plans to break up Allegis.

Ferris did not stand by idly. As part of a major aircraft order for Boeing 747 jets, Ferris offered Boeing $700 million in convertible Allegis notes. This unusual move made Boeing a potential ally for Ferris in any struggle for control of Allegis. Boeing accepted the offer. In late May, Ferris and the Allegis board moved to prepare a special $60 cash distribution for each Allegis share.

By then, however, Ferris had run out of time. He resigned during a contentious board meeting on June 9, 1987. Within days, his successors quietly moved to erase the "Allegis" name forever.

THE TWENTY-FIFTH MAN

For Andy MacPhail, Vice-President for Player Personnel with the Minnesota Twins professional baseball team, the 1986 season held high hopes.[7] In his first full season in charge of the Twins playing roster, MacPhail sought to build on the steady progress made over the 1984 and 1985 seasons by a group of relatively inexperienced players. MacPhail, the players, and Twins fans all expected the team to contend for the American League Western Division championship.

Instead, the season proved to be one long disappointment. After winning three of their first four games, the Twins lapsed into mediocre play that, over the ensuing six months, resulted in a next-to-last-place finish. Their record of 71 wins and 91 losses was the worst Twins performance since a forgettable 1982 season. Twins fans registered their disapproval by staying away from the Humphrey Metrodome, the team's home stadium, in increasing numbers. After two consecutive seasons of record attendance, overall attendance at 1986 home games dropped by nearly 25 percent from the 1985 level.

The Twins also had been surpassed in the division standings by several rival teams whose baseball executives were, like MacPhail, patiently developing rosters of young talent. The combination of sagging attendance and poor team performance invited renewed speculation that, as almost happened in 1984, the Twins franchise might be moved from Minneapolis.

One of the team's major deficiencies in 1986 was pitching. MacPhail shuttled eighteen different pitchers in and out of the ten roster spots normally reserved for pitchers. Many of MacPhail's midseason additions had been marginal performers elsewhere. Unfortunately, they lived up to their reputations while wearing the Twins uniform. The 1986 Twins recorded the worst composite pitching performance of the fourteen teams in the American League.

While MacPhail persevered in his efforts to find a staff of ten competent pitchers, what he chose *not* to do was equally significant. He was permitted under league rules to employ twenty-five players until September 1, yet, in dire need of pitching help, he chose to forgo the twenty-fifth man. As a result, the Twins played the bulk of their disappointing 1986 season with only twenty-four players.

MacPhail was not the only baseball executive to make this choice. In fact, MacPhail and all thirteen of his counterparts in the American League adopted this strategy. Haywood Sullivan of the pennant-winning Boston Red Sox chose to forgo the twenty-fifth man, as did Mike Port of the runner-up California Angels. Dick Balderson, whose Seattle Mariners were the only team with an overall record worse than that of the Twins, also chose the twenty-four man roster. So did Hank Peters, whose Baltimore Orioles finished last in the Eastern Division for the first time. MacPhail, Sullivan, Port, Balderson, Peters, and the others all chose this route, even though their roster needs differed. Sullivan needed a shortstop, Balderson needed catching and defense, Peters desperately sought a third baseman. A twenty-fifth player could have helped each of them.

The team owners—the men and women for whom MacPhail, Sullivan, Port, and the others worked—had agreed in 1968 to a maximum roster of twenty-five players. A 1976 master contract between the owners and the players' union reaffirmed that agreement. That same contract also provided for the possible reduction of rosters by one player. However, the twenty-four man roster was rarely attempted in the ensuing ten years. Certainly, at no other time since 1976 had all teams operated simultaneously with one less player. The owners argued that they could each save over $100,000 annually in salary and travel costs by reducing roster sizes, but these savings made a minor dent in a typical team's operating budget.

Surprisingly, leaders in the players' union only protested mildly. The roster reduction meant that, across the combined American and National leagues, twenty-six players were denied salary and pension opportunities.

On the other hand, the "missing" twenty-fifth man meant more playing opportunities for the remaining twenty-four players on each team.

Still, as spring turned to summer in 1986, and one Twins pitcher after another struggled, MacPhail stuck to his strategy of simply replacing ineffective pitchers, rather than adding one more. The twenty-fifth man was, in baseball parlance, "out for the season" in Minnesota and across the country.

SUMMARY

Our logic for strategy considers persons (a Principle about Persons) taking decisive action (a Principle of Timely Action) on, at a minimum, matters of product quality, employee commitment, and competition (a Principle of Business Basics). The purpose of this chapter has been to introduce four contemporary cases of decisive strategic action. In short, we have written this chapter to show how our logic for strategy helps managers set up strategic problems for analysis and action. We will now consider six different ways to solve those strategic problems.

NOTES TO CHAPTER 2

1. We have been influenced by the arguments made in John Child, "Organizational Structure, Environment and Performance: The Role of Strategic Choice," *Sociology* 6 (1972): 1–22. Child's position has come under fire from a number of prominent management researchers who doubt that strategy has little to do with persons making choices. See, for example, Gareth Morgan, "Rethinking Corporate Strategy: A Cybernetic Perspective," *Human Relations* 36, no. 4 (1983): 345–60, and Jeffrey Pfeffer, *Organizations and Organization Theory* (Boston, Mass.: Pitman, 1982).
2. Strategic ends and means are alike insofar as they are the objects of managers' choices. As we will show beginning in Chapter 3, many strategy models disconnect ends and means, particularly in the context of our Principle of Timely Action, with awkward consequences.
3. Our logic thus serves as an interpretive scheme with which managers can cope with their problems. Our logic, on the other hand, is not a set of scientific truths about objective reality. For an account that explains this distinction, see Richard Rorty, "Texts and Lumps," *New Literary History* 17, no. 1 (1985): 1–16. Rorty's arguments have influenced our entire undertaking here.

4. This case draws upon: Larry Kahaner, *On the Line: The Men of MCI—Who Took on AT&T, Risked Everything, and Won!* (New York: Warner, 1986); Steve Coll, *The Deal of the Century: The Break Up of AT&T* (New York: Atheneum, 1986); and Alvin Von Auw, *Heritage & Destiny: Reflections on the Bell System in Transition* (New York: Praeger, 1983).

5. This case been put together from the following sources: "Texaco and Pennzoil, With Truce Expiring, Again Talk of Settling," *Wall Street Journal*, March 14, 1986, pp. 1, 12; Jennifer B. Hull and Thomas Petzinger, Jr., "Museum's Suit Charges Texaco Violated An Accord Tied to Purchase of Getty Oil," *Wall Street Journal*, May 6, 1986, p. 12; Cary Reich, "The Litigator: David Boies, The Wall Street Lawyer Everyone Wants," *New York Times Magazine*, June 1, 1986, pp. 18–24, 48, 50, 70, 74–76, 84; "Texas Appeals Panel Affirms $9.1 Billion of Pennzoil's Judgment Against Texaco," *Wall Street Journal*, February 13, 1987, pp. 3, 16; Robert A. Bennett, "Winning Friends for Texaco When It Needs Them Most," *New York Times* February 22, 1987, Section 3, p. 6; "Texaco Files Petition for Chapter 11 as Talks with Pennzoil Collapse," *Wall Street Journal*, April 13, 1987, pp. 1, 10; "How Icahn Got Texaco and Pennzoil to Brink of Elusive Settlement," *Wall Street Journal*, December 14, 1987, pp. 1, 13; Thomas C. Hayes, "A $3 Billion Question for Pennzoil," *New York Times*, December 21, 1987, pp. D1, D5; and Stephen Labaton, "Texaco Files to End Bankruptcy," *New York Times*, December 22, 1987, pp. D1–D2.

6. This narrative has been drawn, with the assistance of Erin McGrath, from the following sources: "Rising UAL Turmoil Threatens Ferris' Job as the Chief Executive," *Wall Street Journal*, April 17, 1987, pp. 1, 10; Judith Valente and Scott Kilman, "Pilots May Seek Partner to Buy Parent of United," *Wall Street Journal*, April 27, 1987, p. 6; Laurie P. Cohen, "Trump Sells UAL Stake, Sources Say; Gain May Be More Than $55 Million," *Wall Street Journal*, April 30, 1987, p. 5; Kenneth Labich, "Winners in the Air Wars," *Fortune*, May 11, 1987, pp. 68–79; Scott McMurray and Scott Kilman, "Boeing May Get Stake in Allegis with 747 Order," *Wall Street Journal*, May 13, 1987, pp. 2, 18; Agis Salpukas, "Group With 13% Stake Seeks Allegis Control," *New York Times*, May 27, 1987, pp. 23, 35; Laurie P. Cohen and Judith Valente, "Coniston Presses Battle to Gain Allegis Control," *Wall Street Journal*, June 1, 1987, p. 2; "Allegis Shakeup Came as Shareholder Ire Put Board Tenure in Doubt," *Wall Street Journal*, June 11, 1987, pp. 1, 10; Kenneth Labich, "How Dick Ferris Blew It," *Fortune*, July 6, 1987, pp. 42–46; and Stratford P. Sherman, "The Trio That Humbled Allegis," *Fortune*, July 20, 1987, pp. 52–56.

7. See "The 24-Man Rosters: Is Everybody Happy?", *The Sporting News*, June 23, 1986, p. 12; "24-Man Roster Is Challenged," *New York Times*, May 14, 1986, p. 30; Patrick Reusse, "Twins' Brain Trust Saw Talent Cresting in '86," *The Sporting News*, November 2, 1987, p. 57; *Minnesota Twins*

Media Guide (Minneapolis, 1987); and Dave Sloan, ed., *Official Baseball Guide—1987* (St. Louis: The Sporting News, 1987).

ANNOTATED BIBLIOGRAPHY

A number of entertaining accounts of the Texaco-Pennzoil wrangle and the AT&T divestiture have appeared in the popular press. In addition to those listed in the notes above, these are our favorites:

Coll, Steve. *The Taking of Getty Oil.* New York: Atheneum, 1987.

Petzinger, Thomas Jr. *Oil and Honor: The Texaco-Pennzoil Wars.* New York: G.P. Putnam's Sons, 1987.

Ramsey, Douglas. *The Corporate Warriors.* Boston, Mass.: Houghton Mifflin, 1987.

Shooshan, Harry M., III, ed. *Disconnecting Bell: The Impact of the AT&T Divestiture.* New York: Pergamon Press, 1984.

Temin, Peter, with Louis Galambos. *The Fall of the Bell System.* Cambridge, England: Cambridge University Press, 1987.

Toffler, Alvin. *The Adaptive Corporation.* New York: Bantam, 1985.

Tunstall, Jeremy. *Communications Deregulation: The Unleashing of America's Communications Industry.* Oxford, England: Basil Blackwell, 1986.

3 THE HARVARD POLICY FRAMEWORK

The Harvard Policy framework is a very influential approach to the concept of strategy. Each of the strategy models analyzed in Chapters 4 through 8 depends, to some extent, on the concept of strategy developed at the Harvard Business School beginning in the 1950s. Because the Harvard Policy framework plays such a central role—historically and conceptually—in the development of thinking about strategy, we choose to begin our analysis here.[1] The purpose of this chapter is to introduce, interpret, and critically evaluate the Harvard Policy framework.

THE BASIC IDEAS

The Harvard Policy framework says that strategy is *the pattern of purposes and policies* that defines a company and the businesses in which that company is engaged.[2] The framework leads managers to identify the resources and capabilities of their organizations and to match these resources and capabilities with opportunities and risks present in the business environment. The Harvard model divides strategy into two problems: (1) "formulation" decisions about what to do; and (2) "implementation" decisions about how to execute formulation decisions for business success.[3] The Harvard framework is shown in Figure 3–1.

Figure 3–1. The Harvard Policy Framework.

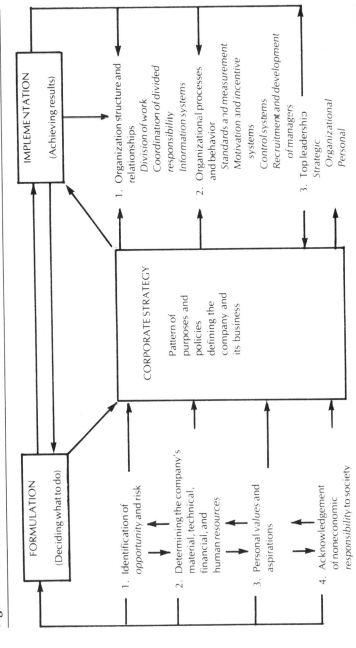

Source: Kenneth R. Andrews, *The Concept of Corporate Strategy*, Third Edition (Homewood, Ill.: Richard D. Irwin), p. 21. Copyright © Richard D. Irwin, Inc., 1987. Reprinted with permission.

Formulation and Implementation

According to the Harvard model, formulation and implementation activities need to be further subdivided into seven categories.[4] In deciding *what to do* a general manager must perform four formulation tasks: (1) identify opportunities where his company may be successful and identify the business risks that are associated with these opportunities; (2) determine the capabilities of the company in terms of material, technical, financial, and managerial resources; (3) assess the personal values and aspirations of the senior executive team; and (4) decide how to fulfill the company's noneconomic responsibility to society. In completing these four tasks, managers articulate a set of decisions and a pattern of policies that will need to be implemented.

In order to *then achieve results* with a strategy formulated in this way, managers must perform three implementation tasks: (5) decide how to structure the organization and coordinate the division of labor; (6) design and implement systems and procedures to accomplish what the organization is going to do; and (7) focus on the leadership necessary to bring about the desired results.

According to the Harvard Policy model, a pattern of purposes and policies emerges from executives' efforts to address these seven tasks.

Managers can better assure desired results for their businesses if they follow a deliberate program of thinking about their companies' strategies. Kenneth Andrews, one of the principals in the Harvard Policy approach, puts the proposition this way: ". . . a business enterprise guided by a clear sense of purpose rationally arrived at and emotionally ratified by commitment is more likely to have a successful outcome, in terms of profit and social good, than a company whose future is left to guesswork and chance."[5] A brief historical review of the Harvard Policy framework will set the stage for our analysis of the model.

A BRIEF HISTORY OF THE HARVARD POLICY FRAMEWORK

The story of the development of the Harvard model is really the story of the development of the Business Policy course in the 1950s and 1960s at the Harvard Business School. Even today in most schools of business, "Business Policy" is the course in which students study corporate strategy and the role of the Chief Executive Officer in shepherding a corporation's strategic efforts.

At the outset, Business Policy was designed as a capstone course in the business school curriculum. It gave students an opportunity to apply knowledge that they had gained in other functional area courses, such as marketing and finance. In Business Policy, functional concepts were applied to corporate-wide problems, usually presented to the student in the form of comprehensive, unstructured case situations. In short, the Business Policy course dealt with the language of business. In studying such functional areas as accounting, marketing, and finance, students learned certain bits of this language. The Business Policy course ensured that each student knew how to move from one part of the language to the other and became a fluent speaker of the language of business.

The early Business Policy course did not use any special diagnostic and evaluative tools peculiar to policy problems per se. Instead, the instructor led students through a basic process of appraising the issues in a case, diagnosing central issues, and recommending courses of action. Students were expected to base their appraisals, diagnoses, and recommendations on the concepts they had obtained in the various functional areas.

In effect, the Business Policy instructor placed the student in much the same role as the old country doctor. By asking the patient some intelligent questions about his symptoms, and by looking back on experience with lots of cases—some of which were like this one in certain relevant respects—the doctor could intuit a course of treatment that would have some chance of working. In this way, the country doctor pieced together a remedy for diphtheria just as the Business Policy student worked out problems of product quality or shifting market demand.

Perhaps the most significant legacy of the early Business Policy course has been the emphasis upon teaching students—and senior executives—to *ask the correct questions* about a strategic problem.[6] As businesses and business environments became more complex, Business Policy faculty at Harvard fashioned a separate, more sophisticated framework that dealt specifically with asking correct questions about policy. That separate framework is what we call the Harvard Policy framework.

AN INTERPRETATION OF THE HARVARD POLICY FRAMEWORK

Strategy is an expansive concept in the Harvard Policy framework. As a pattern of purposes *and* policies, strategy—in this view—encompasses both the ends for corporate activity and the necessary means to achieve these ends.[7] Working with this concept of strategy, the Harvard Policy group members concluded that the processes of shaping strategy—processes known as "strategic management"—were of two fundamental kinds:[8]

1. *Strategy formulation* involved establishing the mission, purpose, and goals for a corporation and then defining a set of appropriate business ventures, methods of competition, and relationships with the company's constituencies.
2. *Strategy implementation* dealt with the subsequent development of organization action plans by which to achieve desired strategic results.

This distinction is both a very basic and a very powerful reminder to managers. Managers must know where the corporation can go and how it can get there for the practice of strategy to make a difference in corporate performance.[9]

Strategy Formulation

The object of strategy formulation, according to the Harvard Policy framework, is to identify an intended future that matches the corporation's strengths and market opportunities while mitigating the corporation's weaknesses and external threats. That intended future must be one that senior managers can pursue in good faith, because it squares with their own aspirations and fulfills the corporation's social responsibilities.[10] With apologies to those who are not sports fans, we can easily illustrate this basic idea by using the great Green Bay Packers professional football teams of the 1960s as an example.

During the glory years of Coach Vince Lombardi, the Packers had key advantages in the quickness and physical strength of their offensive line and the durability of such running backs as Jim Taylor. The famous "Packer sweep," with the guards and tackles leading the way, took advantage of the opportunity to gain yardage in a certain manner. When the environment changed and enemy linebackers and cornerbacks lined up to defend against the "sweep," the Packers created openings for short passes over the middle to gain yardage in a different way. Here, the Packers relied on the accuracy of Bart Starr's passes and the durability and sure hands of receivers such as Max McGee and Boyd Dowler. At the same time, Lombardi avoided "bad strategy" by not relying on Starr's running ability, a relative weakness for the Packers.

In short, the Packers used their strengths to take advantage of opportunities and to defend against threats posed by the opposition. But, notice that there is more to the picture, according to the Harvard Policy framework.

Lombardi, in effect the senior executive for the Packer team, was a stern disciplinarian. Widely known for his belief that winning was "the only thing," Lombardi demanded that Green Bay players adapt to a "Packer way" of playing football. Lombardi's system, a reflection of Lombardi himself, was basic, relentless, and methodical.[11] The Harvard Policy analyst would point to this convergence between Lombardi's values and the Packer playing strategies as one sign of effective corporate strategy.

We can take this point a step further. The Harvard Policy analyst would note that the methodical Packer system made a positive social contribution to the Green Bay, Wisconsin, community. Ownership shares in the Packer corporation were publicly and widely held by citizens of Green Bay and surrounding towns. Thus, as representatives of a small, working-class city, Lombardi and the Packer players contributed to the Green Bay community by exemplifying a "work ethic," a set of values appropriate to the community, according to the Harvard Policy framework.[12]

In sum, the Harvard Policy framework provides one way to understand the strategy formulated by "CEO" Vince Lombardi. Lombardi's strategy, in other words, appears to deal with the important formulation questions set forth in the Harvard approach.[13] As we will now see, the four formulation tasks are designed to prompt managers to ask certain questions about strategy.

Four Formulation Tasks. The four steps in formulating strategy "the Harvard way" include analyses of the: (1) external environment for opportunities and threats; (2) internal strengths and weaknesses of the company; (3) personal values held by senior management; and (4) management's responsibilities to the public. Each analytical task revolves around a central question.

The Harvard model first directs managers to ask: *What environmental trends will affect our company?* In the Harvard framework, these trends are divided among four categories: economic, political, social, and technological. Each of the leading characters in the cases presented in Chapter 2 faces environmental issues of these kinds. Consider these examples.[14]

Economic trends. Following the Harvard approach, William McGowan and Richard Ferris should investigate the economic structures of their respective industries. Both need to examine trends in competition, the demand for substitute products, seasonality in their businesses, industry cost structure, the insensitivity of demand to price changes, and so on. Similarly, the Harvard model calls Hugh Liedtke's attention to global patterns in oil consumption and pricing. Andy MacPhail's economic analyses should logically include national and regional trends in disposable personal income, from which people spend money on entertainment.

Political trends.   In this phase of the Harvard analysis, Ferris and McGowan both must pay attention to present and anticipated public attitudes toward deregulation. With the addition of trans-Pacific air routes, Ferris must follow political events in Japan. Liedtke, of course, cannot ignore what the OPEC ministers are doing. Closer to home, MacPhail should follow Minnesota politics, because the Metrodome stadium is managed by a local government commission.

Social trends.   The Harvard framework points Ferris to "yuppie" lifestyles as they affect travel habits and points Liedtke to changing patterns in commuting and home ownership. McGowan must watch those social trends involving family values and practices. A trend toward more dispersed families bodes well, all else equal, for the long-distance business. MacPhail must understand the effects of changing demographic patterns on baseball attendance and spectator response.

Technological trends.   By now, the Harvard approach to linking environmental trends with business opportunities should be clear. Liedtke needs to follow technological trends in drilling techniques and Ferris should study new aircraft designs. MacPhail needs to understand how baseball pitchers are trained at an early age. And, McGowan must become conversant in fiber optics and superconductivity.

The Harvard framework next directs managers to conduct an internal examination of the company by asking: *Which strategy opportunities is the company capable of pursuing and which opportunities are beyond the company's reach?* This assessment of company strengths and weaknesses requires managers to analyze the material, financial, and human resources available to the company.[15] MacPhail had to consider whether there was sufficient talent (human resources) in the Twins organization to gain a competitive advantage from filling the twenty-fifth roster spot. Liedtke needed to consider the state of Pennzoil's financial resources before deciding to wait out Texaco. In a similar vein, the existence of a separate MCI network (material resources) and the cash flow (financial resources) available from United operations were important factors in the deliberations of McGowan and Ferris, respectively.

Moving to a third formulation task, the Harvard framework prompts managers to ask: *What are the values of the management group and how do these limit or expand the potential choices for a strategy?* According to published accounts, McGowan was driven, in part, by a desire to challenge AT&T.[16] Ferris "grew up" in the hospitality industry and thus arrived at UAL with a perspective that differed from that of other airline executives. Liedtke had grand visions for Pennzoil and stubbornly refused to let Texaco off the hook. MacPhail, in his first major executive position, had already shown a flair for daring moves in assembling the Twins playing roster. The point here is not to conduct extended psychoanalyses of senior executives. Rather, the Harvard model suggests that, as Andrews notes, "We should in all realism admit that the personal desires, aspirations and needs of the senior managers of a company actually do play an influential role in the determination of strategy."[17]

In fact, Andrews goes on to note the "desirability" of this.[18]

The final part of the strategy formulation analysis concerns management's responsibilities to publics other than stockholders. The pertinent question here is: *What program of civic contribution is consistent with both the company's strategic opportunities and social responsibility?* Since the Harvard model was introduced when corporate social responsibility was just becoming a major topic of debate, it was natural to include this issue as part of the framework. McGowan, for example, needs to think about how Execunet and other MCI ventures can be tailored to benefit MCI employees, customers, suppliers, community, governments, and so on. Ferris could consider donating certain Allegis services to those athletes who travel to compete in the Special Olympics, for example. Such a program conceivably assists Allegis's marketing efforts. The Harvard model clearly suggests that executives can gain from a reasoned program of "enlightened self-interest."[19]

All this analytical effort can, of course, be fruitless unless attention is paid to executing grand strategic schemes. With this in mind, the Harvard Policy group specified a series of implementation tasks.

Strategy Implementation

Imagine that you are the first mate on a seventeenth-century sailing ship. One of your tasks is to combine the lookout's reports with your knowledge of the crew's spirit and the captain's habits to recommend, when asked, a plan for engaging an unfamiliar ship or an impending storm. Strategy formulation in the Harvard Policy framework is very much like this. When you and your crew go below deck to ready the cannons, or batten the hatches, however, you engage in different activities. In the Harvard model, these are steps toward strategy implementation.

Strategy implementation deals with organizational action plans designed to bring about the intended future as formulated in the preceding way. In the Harvard Policy framework, implementation is a matter of (1) arranging a set of working relationships (organization structure) appropriate for the strategy; (2) establishing procedures to govern those relationships (organization processes); and (3) adopting a leadership approach that fits the strategy. To the original Harvard Policy framers, a strategy wasn't a strategy until these tasks were accomplished.

The manager designing an appropriate structure must answer such questions as: *How will responsibility be divided? What decisions will be made at what level of management? How will tasks be coordinated? What is the relationship between line and staff organizations, between the headquarters and divisions?* Of the four cases in Chapter 2, perhaps Ferris faced the most perplexing structure issues. He argued fervently that synergies could be produced by combining airline, rental-car, and hotel services. In particular, he painted a picture of customers having their travel reservations processed in one easy stop. Yet, the computerized Hertz, Hilton, and United reservations systems were designed to perform different kinds and volumes of reservations. How to merge these systems was a major implementation issue at Allegis.

Organizational processes and behaviors are the standard operating procedures and routines that define the day-to-day workings of the organization. According to the Harvard framework, if a strategy does not take into account "the way we do things here," it is bound to fail. This phase of the implementation effort guides managers to ask such questions as: *How does the strategy affect each of our important systems and procedures? Do we need new people or new training to achieve these goals? Can the strategy be accomplished within the boundaries of the current incentive and compensation scheme?*

McGowan's plan to enter the residential long-distance market forced him to consider questions of this kind. MCI's salespeople were accustomed to selling to corporate accounts. Reaching the residential customer required new methods, however. Billing practices needed to be revamped as well.[20] Liedtke, on the other hand, had to organize his legal counsel to meet Texaco on the state and Federal levels, as well as to keep track of multiple, concurrent judicial proceedings.

The final piece of the Harvard implementation scheme involves an appropriate leadership approach for a strategy. McGowan must find a way to calm nervous employees, customers, and lenders in the face of DeButts's fury. MacPhail must encourage his fielders and batters as they watch Twins pitchers come and go. Ferris and Liedtke must both assure their constituents that patience with their respective strategies will pay off eventually. Implementation, the Harvard way, requires the deft touch of a leader.

A CRITICAL ANALYSIS OF THE HARVARD POLICY FRAMEWORK

The Harvard Policy framework sends a clear message to managers: strategy formulation without proper attention to implementation is a surefire recipe for disaster. The Harvard group understood that formulation and implementation go hand in hand. Indeed, notice that Figure 3–1 shows the arrows between formulation and implementation running in both directions. Far from being a sequential process, formulation and implementation are logically connected. In the Harvard Policy view, a strategy that cannot be implemented is simply a bad strategy.

There is no doubt that the Harvard Policy framework and the subsequent generations of strategic management models that are its descendants have influenced the way managers choose to run the modern corporation. We now need to assess, from a logical point of view, just how useful the framework can be. Our standards of "usefulness" will be the three principles that make up our logic for strategy (see Chapter 1). *How thoroughly and coherently does the Harvard Policy framework deal with the three principles?*

A Principle about Persons

There is good news and bad news regarding the part persons play in the Harvard Policy framework. The good news comes in two forms. First, the Harvard Policy framers clearly acknowledge that the values people hold are both the reasons for *and* the cause of action. As we will show later, this understanding of values has been lost on many subsequent thinkers about strategy.[21] Second, the Harvard Policy framers astutely observe that the values of key executives must be consistent with a strategy, else these persons will not be able to exercise the leadership needed to carry out the strategy. On both counts, the Harvard Policy model is predicated on a basic understanding of rational action.

The bad news is that the Harvard Policy framers extended this understanding of rational action to a *very limited* cast of characters. The Harvard Policy framework focuses only on the values of a handful of key executives at one company.[22] While this concept of strategy logically follows from a Harvard Business School emphasis on top executive leadership, this limited treatment of rational action is nonetheless a problem.

The issue can be put this way: If the values of senior executives cause their action, don't the values of middle management, lower management, and employees cause their actions as well? According to the Harvard model, we need only look as far as McGowan—but not to his marketing, financial, and technical colleagues—to understand why he and MCI went after AT&T with Execunet. In the same spirit, we need only ask whether Ferris—and not his board members, Hertz executives, and flight attendants, for example—was diligent in his deliberations and comfortable with the Allegis idea.

The Harvard Policy framework arbitrarily isolates the link between values and strategy to those who occupy the executive suite. The reasons for this isolation are never fully explained.[23]

A Principle of Business Basics

On paper, the Harvard framework pays faithful attention to the Principle of Business Basics. The external environment analysis should focus, in the end, on customer needs and wants. The internal analysis should focus on how well these demands are satisfied through the quality and price of products and services. Furthermore, the external analysis is intended to translate competitive trends into a realistic assessment of business opportunities for the company. Rounding out the Harvard approach, the implementation side of the framework should pay almost exclusive attention to employee commitment. However, there are two critical problems with the Harvard Policy approach to "business basics."

First, all strategy formulation and implementation activities take place *within a single company*, according to the Harvard framework.[24] In other words, the only concrete behaviors in Harvard Policy stories take place *within* MCI, insofar as Execunet is concerned, and *within* Pennzoil, insofar as the billion-dollar award is concerned. All other persons and behaviors are aggregated into "the environment" of MCI and Pennzoil. The point of our criticism here is simple: by focusing on a faceless, nameless external environment, and by citing trends rather than concrete behaviors of key individuals, we can easily misapply the framework. Liedtke's problem at Pennzoil provides a clear example of this.

One frequent item found in the environmental analysis behind many strategic plans is a forecast of inflation rates or interest rates. The actual inflation or interest rate is irrelevant for understanding our Principle of Business Basics; the real importance of this information is how it affects the concrete behavior of key competitors and customers. For Liedtke, this means thinking about how McKinley and his successors might factor interest rates or inflation rates into *their* plans. Liedtke needs to ask: If interest rates go down, will McKinley be more inclined to settle the dispute with a cash payment? By not explicitly providing for the translation of trends into expected behaviors, the Harvard framework approach to the external environment analysis can become abstract and misleading.

Second, the "internal environment" of the company is also depicted in the Harvard model as a faceless, nameless entity. Implementation, in this context, becomes a matter of coaxing senior executives to pull the correct "levers" of organization structure, process, and leadership.[25] Employee commitment, in this view, is under the executive's control. Although this assumption is consistent with the Harvard Policy assumption about persons, it probably defies many managers' experiences. It also creates problems when timely action is necessary.

A Principle of Timely Action

We want to caution managers about the strategy formulation–strategy implementation distinction. At first glance, the distinction offers a useful reminder: think before you act. The temptation, however, is to interpret the Harvard framework in this way: implementation only needs to be addressed *after* the fact of formulation. The potential problem with this interpretation can be readily explained in the context of employee commitment.

Suppose that Ferris has faithfully followed the Harvard formulation steps to arrive at the Allegis idea. Now, if he were to worry about employee commitment only after the fact, it would be even harder to gain that commitment, given how novel the Allegis idea was.[26] As a result, it would be more difficult to make Allegis work in a timely fashion.

In short, if managers assume that implementation is only an afterthought to formulation, then the prospects for *timely action* can be dimmed considerably.

Our point here is simple. Employees will become committed more easily to an action if they are somehow included in the *formulation* process. The Harvard framework draws a potentially paralyzing line between the tasks of senior executives (formulation) and middle and lower management and employees (implementation). The chances for undermining the strategy are enormous. In other words, by mistakenly seeing implementation as coming *only after* formulation is completed, managers can turn employee commitment into a frustrating exercise in coercion and persuasion. Timely constructive action is unlikely under those circumstances.

CONCLUSION

The major strength of the Harvard Policy framework is that it gives us a systematic way to ask intelligent questions about a business. The framework defines strategy clearly, points to certain key parameters, and suggests what questions to ask in pursuit of those parameters. Managerial judgment plays a central part in this approach. More importantly, a premium is placed on reasoned analysis of strategic problems, rather than mere intuition and "gut level" reaction.

The Harvard Policy framework is intended to open vistas on the strategic problems managers face. However, the framework also obscures certain vantage points. We have shown how the framework is isolated to the executive suite in a single company. We have also shown how the framework deals quite abstractly with such "business basics" as customers, employees, and competitors. And, we have warned that the separation of strategy formulation and implementation can impede timely managerial action. These are important limitations that must be weighed before applying the Harvard Policy framework.

NOTES TO CHAPTER 3

1. For one historical survey of strategy, see Dan E. Schendel and Charles W. Hofer, "Introduction," in D. E. Schendel and C. W. Hofer, eds., *Strategic Management: A New View of Business Policy and Planning* (Boston, Mass.: Little, Brown, 1979), pp. 1–22. See also Igor Ansoff, *Corporate Strategy:*

Business Policy for Growth and Expansion (New York: McGraw-Hill, 1965), and Peter C. Lorange, *Corporate Planning: An Executive Viewpoint* (Englewood Cliffs, N.J.: Prentice-Hall, 1980).

2. See Kenneth R. Andrews, *The Concept of Corporate Strategy*, Revised Edition (Homewood, Ill.: Richard D. Irwin, 1980), p. 18. Unlike many of his strategy contemporaries, Andrews explicitly defines "strategy" and does so in the context of a business. Many of his contemporaries toss "strategy" about merely as the root for the adjective "strategic." Andrews argues that there is more to a strategy than its connotation of importance.

3. Ibid., pp. 24–28.

4. Ibid., pp. 24–27.

5. Ibid, p. 46. Here, Andrews articulates what amounts to a basic proposition for strategy.

6. There is a temptation to say that a strategy framework is interesting and useful only if it provides some bedrock principles that prescribe actions under various internal and external circumstances. The Harvard Policy framers resisted this appeal to "first principles" about the world and, thus, stand apart from their strategy contemporaries who still search for the scientific truths about strategy.

7. Andrews and company thus apply strategy in a more comprehensive context—that is, means and ends—than do many who have followed them. Schendel and Hofer, for example, arbitrarily separate goals (ends) from means. See Schendel and Hofer, *Strategic Management: A New View of Business Policy and Planning*, pp. 14–18. Andrews can be understood to argue that the means–ends distinction is not readily separable for managers who want to apply strategy to their businesses.

8. See Andrews, *The Concept of Corporate Strategy*, pp. 24–28.

9. The idea that formulating a decision is sufficient pervades much strategy research. It stems from a belief that a strategy is only a set of decisions and that hammering those decisions into some coherent statement is the mark of effective strategy. What's missing, as we will show in Chapter 6, is any sense that other persons at other companies are doing the same thing at the same time! If researchers and managers ignore this, it is no wonder that implementation problems arise.

10. For an analysis of the strengths and weaknesses in this area of the Harvard model, see R. Edward Freeman, Daniel R. Gilbert, Jr., and Edwin Hartman, "Values and the Foundations of Strategic Management," *Journal of Business Ethics* (in press).

11. See Jerry Kramer, with Dick Schaap, *Instant Replay* (New York: World Publishing, 1968); Vince Lombardi, with George L. Flynn, *Vince Lombardi on Football* (Greenwich, Conn.: New York Graphic Society and Wallyn, 1973); Daniel R. Gilbert, Sr., "Vince Lombardi," in *Dictionary of American Biography*, 1988 Supplement (New York: Charles Scribner's Sons, 1988).

12. This approach to social responsibility is set in a larger context in William C. Frederick, "Theories of Corporate Social Performance," in S. Sethri and C. Falbe, eds., *Business and Society: Dimensions of Conflict and Cooperation* (Lexington, Mass.: Lexington, 1987), pp. 142–61. This is a classic example of what Frederick terms "CSR-1."

13. We do not need to know whether Lombardi actually deliberated in this way in order to see the value of this interpretive framework. As noted in Chapter 1, note 18, rational reconstruction efforts are intended to demonstrate the durability—or generalizability—of an interpretation scheme, not whether the process was actually followed in some empirical sense.

14. Here we show one example of the replicability of the Harvard Policy framework questions. See Robert K. Yin, *Case Study Research: Design and Methods* (Beverly Hills, Calif.: Sage, 1984).

15. See Andrews, *The Concept of Corporate Strategy*, pp. 63–71.

16. See Larry Kahaner, *On the Line: The Men of MCI—Who Took on AT&T, Risked Everything, and Won!* (New York: Warner, 1986).

17. See Andrews, *The Concept of Corporate Strategy*, p. 79.

18. Ibid.

19. There is nothing to guarantee, however, that enlightened self-interest squares with commonly held moral rules. See Freeman, Gilbert, and Hartman, "Values and the Foundations of Strategic Management."

20. See Kahaner, *On the Line: The Men of MCI—Who Took on AT&T, Risked Everything, and Won!*

21. This point is central in R. Edward Freeman and Daniel R. Gilbert, Jr., *Corporate Strategy and the Search for Ethics* (Englewood Cliffs, N.J.: Prentice-Hall, 1988), where the authors articulate a Values Principle in Chapter 1.

22. This idiosyncracy is carefully examined in Freeman, Gilbert, and Hartman, "Values and the Foundations of Strategic Management."

23. One possible hypothesis here is that the Harvard Policy framers have yet to work out a coherent theory of the firm.

24. This "self-sufficiency" assumption is commonplace in strategy research. The phenomenon is labeled and documented, in the context of the AT&T divestiture, in Daniel R. Gilbert, Jr., "The Mystery of the AT&T Divestiture," in R. Grover, ed., *Proceedings* (Midwest Academy of Management, 1987), pp. 26–30. In order to get a taste of this theory of the firm, sample Amar Bhide, "Hustle as Strategy," *Harvard Business Review* 64, no. 5 (1986): 59–65, and Pankaj Ghemarvat, "Sustainable Advantage," *Harvard Business Review* 64, no. 5 (1986): 53–58. With such a view of strategy, it is misleadingly easy to blame strategy failures on forces "out there." See, for example, Terence Roth, "Porsche Chief Quits Abruptly as Strategy Fails," *Wall Street Journal*, December 17, 1987, p. 27.

25. It is worth noting that Chester Barnard, to whom many in the Harvard Policy camp pay homage, in 1938 provided a broader perspective on

securing cooperative efforts through bargaining than does Andrews. See the discussion about Barnard and authority in Chapter 1, notes 38–41. The discontinuity in this context says much about the lack of a critical tradition in strategy.

26. This point will be revisited in our Chapter 7 discussion about the effectiveness of planning processes. The Allegis story is stark testimony to the perils of presuming that a firm can be analyzed as an isolated entity.

ANNOTATED BIBLIOGRAPHY

Ansoff, Igor. *Corporate Strategy: Business Policy for Growth and Expansion.* New York: McGraw-Hill, 1965. This book appeared about the same time as the original formulation of the Harvard framework. Ansoff's view of strategy is similar except for a more convoluted process of strategy formulation. Indeed, there is more emphasis on the process of strategic planning than on the development of the content of a particular strategy.

Christenson, C. Roland; Kenneth R. Andrews; Joseph L. Bower; Richard G. Hamermesh; and Michael E. Porter. *Business Policy: Text and Cases*, 5th ed. Homewood, Ill.: Richard D. Irwin, 1982. This casebook contains the best collection of case studies to which the Harvard Policy Framework can be applied, and is the best-selling textbook in the field.

Schendel, Dan E. and Charles W. Hofer. "Introduction." In D. E. Schendel and C. W. Hofer, eds., *Strategic Management: A New View of Business Policy and Planning*, pp. 1–22. Boston, Mass.: Little, Brown, 1979. This article is a history of the development of the field of strategic management. The authors argue that there are three phases: capital budgeting, strategic planning, and strategic management. What we have called the Harvard Policy framework fits into the strategic planning phase.

4 THE PORTFOLIO FRAMEWORK

One common approach to strategy draws heavily on the perspectives of the economist. Economic models of strategy highlight the powerful influence that industry forces can exert on the profitability of a business enterprise.[1] A strategy, in this context, amounts to a plan of action that positions the firm against these industry forces in a certain way. The trick for managers is to find a specific position—or niche—that skews industry forces in the firm's favor in the long term. In this chapter and Chapter 5, we will analyze two well-known economic approaches to strategy.

The Portfolio framework for strategy is specifically designed to apply in cases of business diversification. More often than not, managers at large companies diversify to avoid undue risk and to take advantage of opportunities for growth. A significant part of their corporate strategy deliberations, therefore, focuses on which businesses to pursue and which markets to serve. The best way to decide that is to look at what the company does best and where the opportunities are the greatest. With any luck, those two areas will overlap. A Portfolio framework provides specific guidance for responding to economic forces so that diversification yields a profitable overlap.

Portfolio frameworks come in several flavors. The purpose of this chapter is to introduce the basic theme and three variations and to critically assess the Portfolio framework in light of our logic for strategy. In Chapter 5, we will turn to an economic model, known as the Competitive Strategy framework, developed by Michael Porter at the Harvard Business School. Both economic approaches draw on the general concept of strategy set forth in the Harvard Policy framework. However, the Portfolio and Competitive Strategy frameworks are much more specialized. In these two chapters, we will explore the benefits and costs of that specialization.

THE BASIC IDEA AND VOCABULARY

A diversified firm is simply a portfolio of businesses, according to the Portfolio framework. Individual investors can readily see the analogy to their own securities portfolios. The analogy is no coincidence. According to the capital asset pricing model and similar portfolio models for the individual investor, the best portfolio is that set of securities yielding the combination of risk and expected return that best fits the investor's preferences.[2] For both the individual investor and the corporate portfolio, diversification is pursued to iron out the risk as much as possible without badly hurting the expected return. For most portfolio approaches to strategy, risk reduction for the corporation is a prominent goal.[3]

While the Portfolio framework is ultimately concerned with *corporate* risk and return, the real action in portfolio models takes place within and across the parts of a diversified organization that serve particular markets. These organizational parts are usually called strategic business units, or *SBUs*. The SBU is a core concept in the vocabulary of the Portfolio framework for strategy.

The Concept of Strategic Business Unit (SBU)

An SBU (or business, as it is sometimes called) sells a distinct set of products or services to an identifiable group of customers against competition from a well-defined group of competitors. An SBU must be meaningfully separate from the rest of the organization's businesses, at least in an accounting sense. The function of the SBU is to offer products or services that meet the requirements of the customers who make up the *served* market of that SBU. The SBU is a conceptual tool that managers can tailor to their respective companies.

The SBU concept can be readily understood in the context of our four cases in Chapter 2. Richard Ferris, the Portfolio analyst would point out, began to assemble three basic SBUs in 1985: an airline SBU; a hotel SBU; and a rental-car SBU. Allegis was the name given to this three-part diversified portfolio. The Portfolio framework could help Hugh Liedtke consider the merits of McKinley's proposal to have Texaco buy one, or more, of Pennzoil's businesses as compensation for the Getty dispute. William McGowan's move to unveil Execunet had the effect, in Portfolio framework terms, of adding a residential SBU to MCI's private line SBU. And, although not central to the twenty-fifth man case, the concept of SBU could point Andy MacPhail to the products he delivers to an "in stadium" market and a radio/TV advertising market. In short, "SBU" can accommodate a variety of diversification schemes.

The SBU concept developed in response to the demands of diversification on the concept of strategy. At an organization that competes in many businesses, managers can give only general answers to questions such as: Where are we going? For the diversified company, success requires adaptation to the various markets into which managers intend to sell the company's various products. While a certain identifiable strategic style may mark company activities in every arena, managers probably cannot afford to pursue the same strategy in each one. The concept of SBU thus gives strategy a market-by-market meaning.

The SBU is a response to increasing competition as well. The time is long past when a company could count on having markets largely to itself, or sharing markets in which growth is strong enough to keep everybody happy. For the business strategist, as for the military one, the key to victory is to bring superior resources to bear where your competitor is vulnerable. The way to do that, according to the Portfolio framework, is to find markets in which your particular position and resources make you stronger and to fight your biggest battles there.

Competitive demands, in turn, create organizational ones. Senior executives who want to be responsive to the opportunities in a firm's actual and prospective markets have reason to decentralize, in order to make their managers accountable for selling particular products into particular markets. In other words, senior executives have reason to create SBUs. At the same time, they must be able to monitor performance of the decentralized units and allocate finite corporate resources among them according to the demands created by their appropriate strategic missions. A focus on SBUs sets the stage for these allocation decisions.

Two Dimensions of the SBU

The Portfolio framework is designed to permit both decentralization and adequate control at the senior level by use of a universally applicable way of evaluating a market's prospects and a particular competitor's relative strength in serving that market. The framework provides a clear and pertinent language for organizing analysis of SBUs: the attractiveness of each SBU is a function of *expected market conditions* and *competitive pressures*. Both of these forces reflect economic conditions in an industry.

In the next section, we will introduce three systematic attempts to generate sound strategic options for an SBU. As variations on the Portfolio framework theme, each approach deals with an SBU on the basis of two questions:

1. Market condition question: How favorable is the market served by the SBU and its competitors?
2. Competitive pressure question: How strong is this SBU compared with those against which it competes?

According to all three approaches, the answers to these two questions determine what general strategies make sense for each SBU, how to allocate finite corporate resources among the SBUs, and how the SBUs should be managed. All three approaches concur that relatively strong SBUs serving favorable markets are the greatest long-term producers of wealth for the company. All agree that strong SBUs should be given the resources conducive to rapid growth. All agree that: (1) strong SBUs serving less favorable markets can provide cash needed for growth elsewhere, and should grow and change slowly, if at all; and (2) weak SBUs serving poor markets should be allowed to shrink or—if they are not producing cash—to be eliminated to avoid draining resources that are better used for strong SBUs. In short, each of the three Portfolio variations is a guide to optimal strategies for juggling the portfolio of SBUs that makes up a diversified company.

VARIATIONS ON THE PORTFOLIO
FRAMEWORK THEME

Suppose that Richard Ferris sought to analyze his Allegis strategy with the aid of the Portfolio framework. Three well-known variations available to him are: the BCG Growth-Share Matrix; the PIMS Par ROI model; and the GE Matrix.

The BCG Growth-Share Matrix

The Boston Consulting Group offers its clients the BCG Growth-Share Matrix, whose two analytical dimensions are *market growth rate* and *relative market share*. The basic BCG Matrix assessment of an SBU is this: the faster the growth of the market in which an SBU competes and the greater its share of that market relative to the share of its largest competitor, the stronger the SBU. These two dimensions merit a closer look.

Market Growth and Market Share. The BCG Matrix assumes that, other things being equal, a growing market is a favorable market. The dividing line between a good (i.e., growing) market and a bad one is usually a real sales volume growth rate of 10 percent per year. This is sensible if there is reason to believe that the growth trend will not change suddenly.

From the BCG standpoint, the relevant proxy for competitive strength is market share. BCG stresses the *relative market share* of an SBU. This measure is easily calculated: divide the annual sales of the SBU product by the annual sales of the leading competitor in that market. By this calculation, a relative market share above 1.0 denotes the leader.

The importance of market share in the BCG matrix is predicated on the concept of the *experience curve*. The idea, which goes beyond economies of scale, is that the more that is manufactured of something, the more efficiently it can be manufactured. From this premise, it follows that the biggest competitors in a market are the most efficient. A manager's mission becomes straightforward here: gain market share!

BCG connects market share and profitability by postulating that greater experience over time at manufacturing some product, or providing some service, makes an SBU more efficient at it. The experience curve, thus, seems to be the source of what might be called "historical economies of scale." We will return to this notion later when we critically assess the Portfolio framework as a whole. For now, we only note that the market-share logic in BCG—while more clearly worked out than the growth-rate logic—is also more controversial.

BCG and the Drive for Cash Flow. According to BCG, the main criterion of success for an SBU is cash flow. Whether the time horizon is long or short, the BCG approach can point to a strategy for generating and using cash. The first step is to plot SBUs according to market growth

Figure 4–1. BCG Product Portfolio Chart.

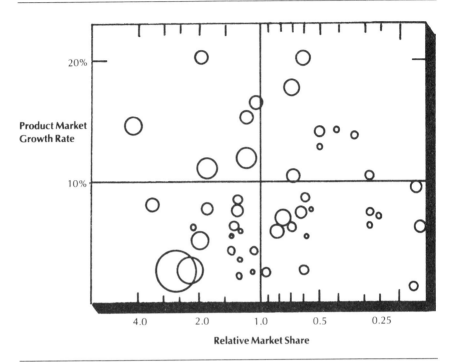

Source: From John S. Hammond and Gerald B. Allan, "Note on the Boston Consulting Group Concept of Competitive Analysis and Corporate Strategy," 9–175–175, page 3. Copyright © 1975 by the President and Fellows of Harvard College. Reprinted by permission of the Harvard Business School.

and market share. Such a "state of the company portfolio" is shown in Figure 4–1 for one diversified company. Each circle represents one SBU. On the basis of such a diagram, the BCG analyst can begin to prescribe action for a company's portfolio.

The BCG Cast of Characters. A relatively strong SBU in a growing market—a Star, in BCG terminology—is destined in the long term to generate a great deal of cash. But, in the short run, it may be a cash user, due to the cash requirements (e.g., capital equipment, inventory, etc.) that growth can command. A Cow SBU, on the other hand, is not expected to grow, and will not need the expensive support that growth requires. Therefore, a Cow will likely generate more cash than a Star. That cash may support some Stars that are not yet self-sufficient.

A Dog, an also-ran in a market of modest or no growth, is worth maintaining in the corporate portfolio only as long as it generates cash. When it does not, the BCG prescription is to shrink or abandon the SBU, rather than resuscitate it. A Question Mark (sometimes called a Problem Child or a Wildcat) is normally a cash user that may, through shrewd action, become a Star and then eventually a Cow. True to the label, however, a Wildcat could amount to no more than a well-behaved Dog. The BCG strategy is to feed this kind of SBU with cash only as long as there is a reasonable prospect of stardom, but to guard against overcommitment. The BCG categories are shown in Figure 4–2.

The punch line for the BCG matrix is straightforward: design your corporate strategy with the strength of the overall portfolio foremost in your mind. Remember that the strongest company is one that has a balanced portfolio, which uses cash from the Cows and Dogs to feed the Stars and the favored Question Marks. By managing the portfolio in this way, the corporation should be self-sufficient in cash and thus be protected from the vagaries of the financial markets.

Figure 4–2.   Categories in the Product Portfolio Chart.

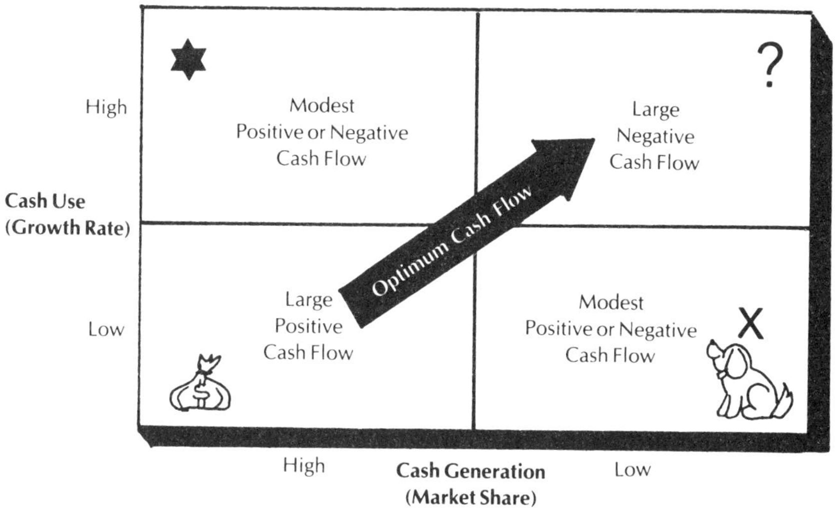

Source: From John S. Hammond and Gerald B. Allan, "Note on the Boston Consulting Group Concept of Competitive Analysis and Corporate Strategy," 9–175–175, page 3. Copyright © 1975 by the President and Fellows of Harvard College. Reprinted by permission of the Harvard Business School.

The BCG approach thus presents a two-edged message to an executive such as Ferris. The good news from BCG is that Ferris can—if United, Hertz, and Hilton can be positioned in a balanced portfolio—outperform the financial markets. The bad news is that Ferris is vulnerable—if a balanced portfolio is not attainable—to having others, namely investors, "redesign" the Allegis portfolio.[4]

The PIMS Par ROI Model

The Profit Impact of Market Strategy (or PIMS) project is truly an ambitious undertaking. PIMS researchers are intent on understanding the determinants of return on investment (ROI) for individual product lines. To that end, they have developed a data base of 1,500 companies and a regression model featuring more than 400 coefficients of return on investment. The most important characteristics of SBUs with good ROIs, according to the PIMS findings, are: (1) market share; (2) relative market share (defined as yours compared to the total of your three largest competitors); and (3) relative product quality.[5] All three characteristics reflect the *competitive strength* of an SBU set against the backdrop of industry economic forces.

To the PIMS researchers, all SBUs are fundamentally alike—and, hence, comparable—on the host of dimensions included in the model. This is a crucial assumption. It means that Ferris, McGowan, Liedtke, and MacPhail could each compare the attractiveness of their respective SBUs with the PIMS norms—hence, "Par" reports—regarding ROI. One widely known Par report compares average ROIs for different combinations of relative market share and relative product quality (measured by R&D as a percent of sales). That Par report contains two clear implications:

1. Where relative market share is high, spending on R&D does not make a great deal of difference; ROIs will be high any way.
2. Where relative market share is low, the less R&D spending the better.[6]

On both counts, PIMS and BCG have familiar rings. In essence, this particular set of PIMS findings suggests that: (1) R&D spending can be redundant where experience-curve effects are significant; and (2) R&D spending can be a waste of resources where competitive position is weak. These are, to be sure, only a small subset of the conclusions drawn by PIMS analysts.

PIMS and BCG approach the portfolio problem from different perspectives. Unlike PIMS, BCG emphasizes cash rather than ROI, perhaps because the BCG analyst assumes that generating cash from operations is always preferable to borrowing. Partly for that reason, BCG also places stronger emphasis than PIMS on the health of the whole company, which is sustained by a proper balance of cash generators and cash users. BCG sees value in limiting borrowing.

Still, on the whole, PIMS supports the BCG model. In some respects PIMS makes modifications that improve BCG rather than undermine it.[7] For example, there is some evidence that the average Dog does generate cash, even more than the amount used by the average Question Mark of comparable size.[8] So, the "harvest" of a Dog SBU may be a long and bountiful one. PIMS also supports BCG's recommendation that managers at SBUs harvest high market share early in the product's history—when market share is easier to get—and that only later should market share be sacrificed for cash. In short, PIMS is a body of statistical evidence that, in many cases, sharpens the intuition upon which BCG is predicated.

The GE Matrix

One of the most celebrated efforts at devising a Portfolio framework is the General Electric approach. In 1972, executives at GE, with the consulting assistance of McKinsey and Company, designed a three-by-three matrix which, like PIMS, addressed SBUs from the perspective of investment attractiveness. The GE/McKinsey approach to business was no mere planning gimmick. GE executives, in the spirit of the framework, partially reorganized the company to create a number of SBUs, each with its own plans and planning manager. GE was actually a laboratory for the "technology" of Portfolio strategy.[9]

The GE matrix pointed managers to a number of indices for "business strength" (competitive strength of the SBU) and "industry attractiveness" (market attractiveness). Like its predecessors, the GE matrix generates specific strategy recommendations for the portfolio. Businesses in the most attractive areas should aggressively seek growth and bigger market share for long-term profits. Those on the "middle ground" must seek profit now and for the foreseeable future. Managers of businesses in the worst area should minimize investment in capital equipment and research and development, and need not try to retain market share. Instead, they are advised to aim at cash flow for the near term, which may be the only term left. As a rough guideline, we might interpret the GE matrix as saying that an SBU of above-average competitive strength should try to grow faster than its market while a below-average SBU should try for slower growth. The GE analyst would likely counsel McGowan, on this basis, to tread carefully with Execunet, given AT&T's dominance. The same analyst would caution Ferris about United's competing head-to-head with Texas Air. These strategic postures, along with the key GE indices, are depicted in the GE/McKinsey Screen in Figure 4–3.

The matrix technology changed the way GE was managed. For one thing, abandoning a business was no longer a sign of failure and cowardice. Managers were assigned—and rewarded for achieving—financial and nonfinancial objectives consistent with the matrix locations of their SBUs. GE executives gradually learned to delegate essential parts of planning to the SBUs while still permitting top managers to add value to the process from their company-wide perspective on the portfolio.

The BCG, PIMS Par, and GE approaches are designed to be variations on the Portfolio framework theme. At the same time, each approach

Figure 4–3.   The GE/McKinsey Screen.

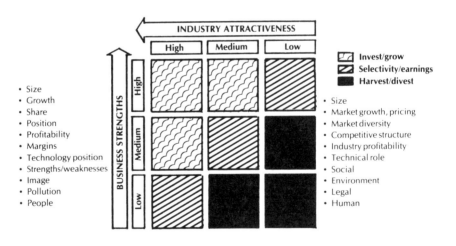

Source: McKinsey & Company, Inc., New York. Reprinted with permission.

presents a more narrowly focused set of strategy variables than does the Harvard Policy framework. One important test, then, is how useful these variables are for management activities. As we will now see, there are some significant problems with Portfolio approaches. Once again, these problems can be highlighted in the context of our logic for strategy.

A CRITICAL ANALYSIS OF THE PORTFOLIO FRAMEWORK FOR STRATEGY

Parsimony is clearly one attribute of the Portfolio framework for strategy. Using a mere handful of concepts, the Portfolio strategist attempts to make some specific claims that apply across the diverse business endeavors of McGowan, Liedtke, Ferris, and MacPhail alike. Unless millions of individual portfolio investors are wrong, searching for a balanced portfolio is a concise and durable idea. The key question, however, is how well the notion of portfolio management can be summarily transferred from the individual level to the domain of corporate strategy.

A Principle About Persons

One feature of all Portfolio strategy approaches should be immediately apparent. There are no persons in these accounts of strategy. Put in different words, managers are incidental to the Portfolio framework for strategy. Thus, unlike the Harvard Policy framework, the Portfolio models give passing attention, at best, to our Principle about Persons.

It is certainly true nonetheless that the Portfolio framework *suggests* a role for persons. The GE matrix is a case in point. Implicit there is the idea that the matrix can be used to set individual managers' objectives and reward their performance in ways appropriate to the strategic situation. By this logic, SBU managers in the growth area should be measured and rewarded by growth targets primarily, and profit secondarily. In the middle area, profit is the primary measurement. In the Dog area, cash flow may be the best index. To run a Cow, a manager must be adept at long-term asset stewardship, in order to maintain appropriate inventory relative to sales, low manufacturing costs, and high productivity. A Wildcat manager will likely be rewarded largely by salary rather than incentive compensation, if the corporation's executives want to signal a commitment to risk-taking and a tolerance of occasional failure. At Norton Company, executives actually tailor rewards to the strategic situation: there are more than fifty types of incentive plans for SBU managers. Each is designed for a different part of the matrix.[10]

One of the more difficult tasks for corporate managers is to make division and SBU managers content with their allocation of capital and other limited resources. Showing an SBU manager how the strategy for his or her unit fits into, and is justified by, the plans of the organization as a whole may not end all dissatisfaction. However, if the standards of performance for the unit and its managers are appropriate and fair, SBU managers may accept not being responsible for the glamorous Stars or daring Wildcats.

Different strategic areas ought to attract managers of different styles and personalities. The visionary, charismatic entrepreneur like McGowan or Ferris would be most appropriate to the growth strategy. The efficiency-minded bureaucrat, who is always asking subordinates what they have done for him lately, best suits the matrix area where the future is short and a change of strategy will cost too much and have little effect. It is all too common for corporate managers to "reward" the successful manager of a small, but growing, business with a job as head of a large SBU. If that SBU does not need innovation and growth, the results can be disastrous for everybody except the competition.[11]

Our point is that, on each of these counts, the Portfolio framework hints that complex issues involving persons always accompany portfolio analyses. Yet, the Portfolio framework is silent on these issues. Great strategies will fail if those accountable for their execution are disaffected or just not capable. The Portfolio analyst, upon reflection, will admit that we must look elsewhere for those solutions.

A Principle of Business Basics

On paper, the Portfolio framework for strategy merits high marks for paying attention to customers, product quality, and competition. (On matters of employee commitment, we will defer our analysis to "A Principle of Timely Action.") Yet, there are some strong reasons to be skeptical here. In particular, a number of assumptions about "business basics" in the Portfolio framework are incomplete, unclear, or both. We will examine four points in this regard.

Competition.   Neither the BCG nor GE matrix deals with the ways in which one competitor's actions may affect others' actions. The BCG matrix is a tool available to anyone. Why then should any SBU manager assume that it is possible to gain a strategic advantage by using the same matrix any competitor can use? Portfolio approaches, in other words, do not help us understand what happens when McKinley and Liedtke both use the same matrix to outposition each other.

Of course, managers can aim for a greater market share. But what if similarly placed competitors have the same objective? Market share is, by definition, a finite resource. The standard use of the matrix, in effect, understates an essential fact about strategy in war or business: adversaries react to what others do. It is necessary, therefore, to see how competitors use the matrix, how they commit their resources, and how their array of SBUs constrains their ability to commit resources to certain markets.[12] The Portfolio framework is of little help in identifying competitors' deliberations.

SBUs, Markets, and Conceptual Precision.   A Portfolio framework for strategy places a premium on a manager's ability to distinguish different market segments and different product lines—and, hence, SBUs. Accordingly, a key test for the Portfolio framework is how clearly it helps managers define possible market opportunities and the SBUs to serve those markets. Consider the hypothetical Fenwick, Inc., in this regard.

Fenwick, Inc., makes only institutional (e.g., restaurant) electric ranges, all one model, and sells them all in the New York metropolitan area. It is therefore a single-SBU company. Fenwick makes 6 percent of the stoves sold in North America, 28 percent of the stoves sold in the New York metropolitan area, 21 percent of the electric ranges sold in North America, 37 percent of the institutional electric ranges sold in the New York metropolitan area. For the purposes of the BCG matrix, what is Fenwick's market share? The question is a serious one. Depending on the answer, Fenwick might be Star or Question Mark, Cow or Dog, and Fenwick executives would need to design a strategy accordingly.[13] Yet, this is not the only question Fenwick executives must ask in looking at their business.

They must ask: Where does Fenwick's competition come from? "From similar products" is the standard answer. But, similar in what way? Fenwick executives might stipulate that competing products are all products that any customer would consider buying instead of the Fenwick product. Are gas ranges among Fenwick's competitors? Microwave ovens? Does Fenwick have separate SBUs for restaurants and other institutions? For retail and wholesale markets? For the New York area and others? In short, distinguishing SBUs on the basis of customer types is both complex and crucial. Managers who contemplate using the Portfolio framework—and, hence, the SBU concept—need to justify separate SBUs on the basis of customer and market characteristics.[14]

These are not rhetorical questions, nor are they unanswerable. Managers who want to make good use of an SBU-based approach to strategy must sometimes find and defend good answers to those questions, or else risk being misled by the matrices they use.

The BCG, PIMS, and GE tools are not sources of ultimate truths about how to define and manage SBUs.[15] These approaches can provide only general guidance about positioning the hypothetical Fenwick, for example. Portfolio models are preliminary, not absolute. With regard to "business basics," the Portfolio framework provides one way to categorize the effects that customers and competitors—two "business basics"—can have on strategy. In short, the Portfolio framework is geared toward helping managers make general and constrained choices, rather than discoveries, about market segments. This guidance is fine, as far as it goes. However, it is limited when we ask for advice about how to understand SBUs in the context of industry forces and how to gain market share.

Making Sense of SBUs in the Industry Context.   Each of the Portfolio approaches discussed above draws sharp distinctions among the generic strategies available to SBU managers and corporate portfolio managers alike. Accordingly, the Portfolio strategy framework places a premium on the exactness by which the two central analytical dimensions—market conditions and competitive position—can be interpreted. Portfolio strategists set themselves up for potential problems in this regard.

What makes a market attractive is a controversial issue. The standard applications of the Portfolio matrix ignore such structural features as barriers to entry, intensity of competition, the possibility of substitution, the relative power of suppliers and buyers, and the agenda of government agencies and other interested parties. As we will argue in the Chapter 5, these are important matters for whole industries, matters that will surely affect some or all of the markets within the industry. If a market is very unfavorable in any of these ways, it may be a very hard place to make any money, as McGowan and Ferris painfully realized.

This point about market indices is a complication for the matrix technology, but, except in the case of the BCG matrix, not a serious flaw. These features can be incorporated into the indices of market attractiveness (the GE dimension), but not so readily into indices of market growth (the BCG dimension).

It is not so easy to fix the indices of competitive strength. The standard Portfolio matrices allow the indices to be weighted differently in different markets, because marketing is a key success factor in this business, distribution in that one, service availability in another, and so on. However, within a business the success factors may change as the market changes. Technological superiority may matter early, packaging and promotion later, and low production overhead last in a mature market. We can understand MacPhail's problems with pitching (technology) in this light, while Ferris initially had to package Allegis coherently before returning to overhead (labor costs) issues.

Much of the value of the PIMS program is based precisely on evidence that different characteristics of SBUs are advantageous at different points in the life of a market. Research has shown that product quality and efficiency in the use of resources are very important in mature businesses, but the evidence is weak for new markets.[16] If government policy changes or is likely to change, the lobbying function may suddenly become paramount. In this context, McGowan had clear reason to worry about lobbying first and, only later, technological changes in MCI's network. The indices of competitive strength must be chosen on a case-by-case basis and changed with time. If so, then certain changes in the environment may change not only the importance of some of the indices, but also the pecking order of some of the competitors.

Blurred Dimensions.   There is a more fundamental problem with the two-dimensional logic of the Portfolio framework.

Although market attractiveness is theoretically independent of competitive strength and not affected by competitors' strategies, the fact is that a strong competitor can make a market more or less attractive. When Prego spaghetti sauce became a national brand, the market expanded enormously, and expanded even further when Prima Salsa executives attacked Prego's position and Prego executives retaliated.[17] The possibility that market attractiveness and competitive position can interact is a serious complication for SBU and portfolio executives. Portfolio models do not distinguish between a highly fragmented market and one with four or five competitors. Whether to assess the position of your SBU by its absolute percentage of market share or by its share relative to other large competitors is a judgment call, one that the approach does not help us make. Even if these problems in specifying SBU contexts could be solved, there is a more basic issue involving the Portfolio approach to "business basics."

Experience Curves and the Grail of Market Share.   The lure of, and search for, market share looms large in the BCG approach and plays some role in every Portfolio model. As we noted above, the route to market share is paved with the experience of a company in producing a product more efficiently over time. BCG analysts claim to have evidence that this "experience curve" can be extended to other costs—distribution, advertising—as well. All costs, they say, drop 20 percent or more each time volume doubles.[18]

Significant early support for the claim came from wartime airframe manufacture, and from Alcoa's manufacture of aluminum products. BCG consultants finally became convinced of it by noting that Texas Instruments made a great deal of money in pocket computers by taking market share. To date, however, no careful, long-term, broad-based analysis is available to support the hypothesis.[19] Economists have done a great deal of analysis on the issue of the experience curve, and they have not reached any consensus.[20] Statistical evidence for the BCG version of the Portfolio approach is hard to find, in any case. Those who compile data seldom do it by SBU. Even if these investigations were to confirm the experience curve, however, there are two intuitive problems with the concept.

First, it is not patently obvious that the length of relevant experience is determined by the age of the SBUs. When executives at Procter & Gamble start out to sell a new consumer product, P&G has essentially no market share. But, P&G managers know a few things before the game even begins. When IBM went into personal computers, the company was no babe in the woods. IBM executives had experience in most of the important facets of the business. The same point can be made for Ferris and United's trans-Pacific route entry.

Second, the historical economies of experience curves can obscure an important matter in the present. The economies achieved will still depend in part on the minimum efficient scale, which varies from industry to industry. We know that it is cheaper to manufacture a quarter of a million cars per year than to manufacture a hundred. It is not so clear that it is cheaper to manufacture a million a year, much less ten million in ten years. The key point is this: the corporate experience curve may describe the *wrong* kind of learning. After all, what is the advantage of long experience with an outdated, inefficient technology? The story of Bethlehem Steel in the late 1960s is a vivid illustration.[21] This potential fallacy of historical economies is actually the manifestation of a still more fundamental issue: Is more market share always preferable? There are, again, intuitive reasons for responding "no."

Market share certainly creates awareness of and credibility for a brand name, bargaining power for its producer, and a healthy respect for the company that has the greatest clout with buyers. These advantages do not have much to do with the experience curve, but they are advantages of market share all the same. It does not follow, however, that SBUs with higher market share perform better. Many managers have seen how large SBUs, much less large companies, can become unwieldy, overconfident, and averse to innovation.

Sometimes there are disadvantages to high market share. A larger SBU may be harder to manage effectively, whether or not managers trained to manage by the numbers realize it. Constraints on supply—a critical matter in certain industries—are usually more serious for a larger SBU. Once market share is great enough, it may invite the unwelcome attention of some hostile parties, possibly including the Justice Department.[22]

Michael Porter has argued that low market share can be as advantageous as high, and better than a medium share.[23] The small competitor can find a niche for his differentiated product and so avoid direct competition with the giants, which profit by dominating the larger market. McGowan and other private-line suppliers began this way. The medium-size firm, by contrast, is too small to dominate a market and too large to hide in a safe segment. These scenarios set the stage for our main point here.

Nothing in the BCG approach, or Portfolio models in general, is of much help in deciding whether the value of additional market share exceeds the cost of getting it. Market share is supposed to be worth the price early in the product life cycle, but not later. However, that statement is a vague and general one. Ferris and McGowan both knew that the obvious way to increase market share was to buy it: lower prices and thereby sacrifice current profits to future ones. However, that strategy may trigger retaliation from competitors—Texas Air and AT&T, respectively—better equipped to fight a price war. Sometimes, too, the temptation to lower prices is rudely accompanied by the realization that it's not always possible to raise them again. Sophisticated strategic thinking of this kind is mandatory for McGowan, Liedtke, Ferris, and MacPhail, yet the Portfolio models are silent on these matters. That silence hints at how the Portfolio strategy framework deals with timely action.

A Principle of Timely Action

The Portfolio strategy framework deals with timely action in a curious way. Whereas the individual investor looks to a securities portfolio as a way to smooth risk over the ebb and flow of market events, the Portfolio strategy analyst takes a decidedly static view.

This point is crystal clear in the context of employee commitment and strategy implementation. As one of our colleagues has phrased it, "Implementation just happens" in the world of Portfolio strategy.[24] There are no organization charts to draw or redraw in the Portfolio strategy; no disputes among SBU managers over resource allocations and SBU objectives; no mechanisms for matching executives' skills and values to different SBU contexts. In a world without implementation problems, timely action is irrelevant. So it is with the Portfolio approach to strategy.

This is not to suggest that timely action could not have a central place in the various Portfolio frameworks. Suppose that the fictional Colossal Conglomerate Company had an SBU with a second-best market share in a market growing at 9 percent per year.

According to the BCG matrix, an SBU with the second-best market share in a market that is growing at 9 percent per year is poorly placed for *both* competitive strength and market attractiveness. As a Dog, the SBU is a bad candidate for investment and a dubious proposition for survival. That rule dooms most SBUs and, if the Portfolio analyst is serious about timely action, should be relaxed. One friendly amendment to it would link market attractiveness to the product's life cycle in a way that does not call anything under 9 percent growth the end of the line.[25]

The BCG matrix does not depend on product life cycle, but some BCG users do. So do users of some of the successor matrices that try to improve on BCG by addressing the time-related shortcomings we have mentioned. According to the consensus about life cycles, the less "mature" the market that the SBU serves, the better are the conditions for expanding and capturing market share. The problem here is the risk attached to being first with the most. Aside from early uncertainties about whether there is going to be a substantial market at all, an SBU manager might gear up rapidly with what turns out to be a relatively inefficient technology, only to be stuck with it for a long time. Some companies—IBM, according to some sources—achieve great success by always waiting until the market settles down before they enter it.[26]

In any case, it is sometimes hard to know until too late what stage the market is in. A hot seller may be just a fad. Or, if not a fad, it may move through all the stages much faster than expected—an increasingly frequent occurrence. And, markets may actually improve through the discovery of new uses or new users for the product, and through outside events (e.g., something OPEC does) that give the product more value. The attractiveness of the coal market, for example, changed overnight.[27]

Equally unpredictable is the effect of new technology on the market. McKinsey and Company has suggested that technologies have characteristic S-shaped life cycles. At first, the progress afforded by the technology is slow. Then it accelerates dramatically before finally dropping off. As the first technology is hitting its stride, a new one is just starting to make a difference. The trick is to move at just the right moment from the old technology to the new. However, this can be an expensive and sometimes traumatic movement.[28]

The upshot is this: the Portfolio strategy framework provides little guidance for strategy implementation—and, hence, employee commitment—and the timing of portfolio additions, subtractions, or neither. If asked for advice about timely action, the Portfolio analyst will, upon reflection, have to admit that there is no place for discussion of timing in the framework.

CONCLUSION

There is nothing inherently objectionable about a strategy framework that has to be applied with a dose of common sense. A strength of Portfolio strategy frameworks, in general, is that these models leave considerable room for autonomy in executive action. Portfolio strategy models are concise interpretations of the problems and opportunities that go with a diversified business. Portfolio strategy models suggest quite clearly that management action makes a major difference in distinguishing a firm from the norm in each generic, industry setting.[29]

On the whole, then, thoughtful use of the matrices helps managers understand the constraints facing them and the need to work with or around them. The matrices do not provide any evidence for the view that strategy is trivial. They do teach something about how little strategy can mean if it is designed inappropriately for the circumstances.

Some critics seem to have the matrices in mind when they complain that today's managers manage by the numbers, inferring that these managers do not understand the fundamentals of the company's business. These managers, the critics maintain, delude themselves into thinking that they only have to look at a matrix to determine how to allocate resources to a portfolio of SBUs.[30]

The same critics and others decry short-term goals and measures as encouraging the tactics that undermine the company in the long run. Critics blame an excessive concern with the current status of current SBUs, making the matrix framework the scapegoat.

We do not entirely agree with these criticisms. The matrices do not claim to provide *all* the information needed to manage a corporation. A weak manager may use them as a crutch, and so ignore other important information. However, there is no reason to believe that a manager who does that would be any better off without them. Nor do the matrices force attention on just the short term. If they are used correctly, they do take into account the long-term prospects of the markets that the SBUs serve. Recall that the indicated strategy for a Star SBU is to get market share in the long run, even at the sacrifice of current profits.

In one way, though, this criticism does not entirely miss. In the long term, the enterprise does not prosper or even survive by succeeding in the markets it serves or by leveraging the resources it has available at any given time. For the very long haul, executives must prepare to enter new markets and to acquire resources not now on hand. The matrices give no guidance there. More to the point, they seem to oppose new SBUs, which must begin with no market share, but which sometimes justify, and may even require, great resources and great patience.

Users of the Portfolio strategy framework must be prepared to apply *huge* doses of common sense and invest in other understandings as well. This preparation is necessary simply because concrete actions by managers, customers and competitors are, at best, tangential to the Portfolio framework. Consequently, the Portfolio strategy framework evades our Principle about Persons and Principle of Timely Action. This, in turn, limits what the Portfolio analyst can rightfully say about our Principle of Business Basics. In the end, there is room for doubt as to whether the portfolio concept can be directly transferred from the individual investor's hands to those of the CEO without considerable enhancement. As we will show in Chapter 5, the logical problems with the Portfolio strategy framework do not necessarily limit the general usefulness of economic approaches to strategy.

NOTES TO CHAPTER 4

1. The firm's environment, on this view, is a composite of parameters that are assumed to reflect all the relevant activities of customers, competitors, suppliers, government officials, and other assorted kibitzers who can affect the firm. Against this backdrop, the strategist's task is similar to the meteorologist's task. Both attempt to read the "correct" patterns of external forces with sufficient foresight so that they can avoid being surprised.

2. For the canonical version of the capital asset pricing model, see H. M. Markowitz, *Portfolio Selection: Efficient Diversification of Investments* (New York: John Wiley, 1959). Remember that, in spite of the enlightenment provided by thinking of a diversified company as a portfolio of stocks, this analogy, like any other, can be misleading. To begin with, chief executives are doing more than buying and selling stocks.

3. Why does diversification within a corporation provide advantages for a stockholder who has the option of reducing risk by diversifying his or her personal portfolio? The assumptions—not justified in the case of a poorly managed company—are that risk reduction can be accomplished more efficiently within a firm than by each stockholder individually, and that the firm can reduce transaction costs in cash flow transfer and achieve economies in management, administration, marketing, and technology. See Malcolm S. Salter and Wolf A. Weinhold, *Diversification through Acquisition: Strategies for Creating Wealth* (New York: Free Press, 1979).

   Aside from the interests of the stockholders, however, managers of diversified firms have reasons for not wanting the companies they manage to fail as a result of insufficient resources, or to be acquired as a result of superabundant resources relative to investment opportunities. For a positive, though not uncritical, view of diversification and a sympathetic understanding of those who have to manage it, see Milton Leontiades, *Managing the Unmanageable* (Reading, Mass.: Addison-Wesley, 1986). Rumelt famously argues that greater relatedness among the corporate businesses correlates positively with profit. See Richard P. Rumelt, *Strategy, Structure, and Economic Performance* (Boston, Mass.: Division of Research, Harvard Business School, 1974).

4. Note that the tools for managing the Allegis portfolio were not under Ferris's proprietary control. The Coniston partners certainly had access to the portfolio through their market activities.

5. See the *PIMS Program Data Manual* (Cambridge, Mass.: The Strategic Planning Institute, 1977 and other years).

6. See Derek F. Abell and John E. Hammond, *Strategic Market Planning* (Englewood Cliffs, N.J.: Prentice-Hall, 1979) for a summary of individual and combined findings.

7. For an extended comparison of the two, see Noel Capon and Joan Robertson Spagli, "A Comparison and Critical Examination of the PIMS and BCG Approaches to Strategic Marketing Planning," Harvard Business School Case 578-148,1978.

8. For an essay about profitable Dogs, see Donald C. Hambrick and Ian C. MacMillan, "The Product Portfolio and Man's Best Friend," *California Management Review* 25 (1983): 84–95. For helpful insights into the scope and limits of portfolio matrices, see Donald C. Hambrick, Ian C. MacMillan, and Diana L. Day, "Strategic Attributes and Performance in a BCG Matrix—A PIMS-Based Analysis of Industrial Product Businesses," *Academy of Management Journal*, 25 (1982): 510–31, and Donald C. Hambrick and Ian C. MacMillan, "The Association between Strategic Attributes and Profitability in the Four Cells of the BCG Matrix—A PIMS-based Analysis of Industrial-Product Businesses," *Academy of Management Journal* 25 (1982): 733–55.

9. For a history of the development and implementation of the GE matrix, see Francis J. Aguilar and Richard G. Hamermesh, "General Electric: Strategic Position—1981," Harvard Business School Case 381-174, 1981.

10. See Robert Cushman, "Norton's Top-Down, Bottom-Up Planning Process," in M. Leontiades, ed., *Policy, Strategy, and Implementation* (New York: Random House, 1983), pp. 160–72. The article is a description of Norton's planning process from the vantage point of the chief executive officer of the company. Though many companies make some use of a portfolio matrix, there are few that have taken matters so far as to tie management compensation to it. See Philipe Haspelagh, "Portfolio Planning: Uses and Limits," *Harvard Business Review* 60, no. 1 (1982): 58–73 for an account of the spread of matrix technology in American companies.

11. Psychologists working with strategists have had some success in matching personalities to strategies. Macomber, for example, did personality assessment in support of strategy in diversified companies. See William Macomber, "Red, Yellow, and Green Managers," (Philadelphia: Hay Associates, 1978).

12. There are some lesser known offspring of the major matrices that address this issue. For example, the Directional Policy Matrix, a Shell invention, is designed to take account of competitors' positions and strategies and recommend actions accordingly. In some cases, it is possible to look at a competitor's entire array of SBUs to see what commitments of corporate resources are possible in the areas of interest. See John H. Grant and William R. King, *The Logic of Strategic Planning* (Boston, Mass.: Little, Brown, 1982).

What all the SBU matrices obscure, however, is the extent to which strategy can be seen as a game-theoretical matter. What an SBU does must, if its manager is rational, be a function of what the competitor is expected to do, and vice versa, with the result that calculation of an optimal strategy may be complex and subtle, or simply impossible. The SBU matrices characteristically aggregate the competition rather than encourage careful attention to each competitor's view of the strategic situation and probable response to it. See note 1. Ironically, it is BCG's Bruce Henderson himself, more than any other strategist, who has been eloquent about the necessity to be sensitive to a competitor's intentions and try to affect them. The BCG matrices are of very little help in that crucial process, and on the whole do not accommodate the notion that game theory offers a way to analyze strategy.

In depicting strategy as a matter of deliberating about someone else's deliberations, Henderson rightly puts himself in opposition to those who see little or no place for the "rational model" of corporate management. See Jeffrey Pfeffer, *Organizations and Organizational Theory* (Boston, Mass.: Pitman, 1982), for a treatment sympathetic to those critics of the notion that deliberation is essential to what managers do.

13. A clever defender of the BCG matrix can always explain the apparent success of a Dog by redefining the market to make it a Cow. So whatever cash flow there is turns out to be just what one would expect. One sure sign of a useless theory is that it can be interpreted so that any possible event confirms it. As a practical matter, the theory is likely to be useless in the hands of those who always interpret it so that any actual event confirms it. The same might be said of many consulting tools.

14. The law sometimes works out coherent and defensible ways of individuating things for practical purposes, but the body of antitrust decisions gives little guidance on how to divide a company into SBUs. For the most part, the application of antitrust laws appears to make the possibility of substitution the broadest definition of a market, and to define a market segment according to differences in price, distribution, and customers served. Similar cases have been treated differently, however. One company is nailed for dominating a market defined narrowly, while another gets off because it has a small share of a broadly defined market. For details, see Robert D. Buzzell, "Note on Market Definition and Segmentation," Harvard Business School Case 579-083, 1978.

15. For an influential criticism along these lines and other lines as well, see Robert H. Hayes and William J. Abernathy, "Managing Our Way to Economic Decline," *Harvard Business Review* 58, no. 4 (1980): 67–77. Not all readers will agree with their argument in every particular, but nobody interested in either the theory or the practice of strategy can afford not to read it.

16. See Hambrick, MacMillan, and Day, "Strategic Attributes and Performance in a BCG Matrix—A PIMS-Based Analysis of Industrial Product Businesses."

17. See Howard Rudnitsky, with Jay Gissen, "Chesebrough-Pond's: The Unsung Miracle," in M. Leontiades, ed., *Policy, Strategy, and Implementation* (New York: Random House, 1983), pp. 209–17.

18. See Bruce D. Henderson, *Henderson on Corporate Strategy* (Cambridge, Mass.: Abt Books, 1979). Henderson appears to be the person most responsible for development of the BCG matrix.

19. See Kenneth M. Davidson, *Megamergers: Corporate America's Billion-Dollar Takeovers* (Cambridge, Mass.: Ballinger, 1985).

20. Joe S. Bain, *Industrial Organization* (New York: John Wiley, 1959), and F. M. Scherer, *Industrial Market Structure and Economic Performance* (Chicago: Rand-McNally, 1970) are two examples. They are among the leaders in the field of industrial organization economics, and some familiarity with their work would be useful to anyone interested in any sort of corporate or SBU strategy.

21. For a very readable introductory account, see John Strohmeyer, *Crisis in Bethlehem: Big Steel's Struggle to Survive* (Bethesda, Md.: Adler & Adler, 1986). See also "Let's Hear It from the Winner—and from a Loser," *Fortune* (January 18, 1988): 38–9.

22. See Paul N. Bloom and Philip Kotler, "Strategies for High Market-Share Companies," *Harvard Business Review* 53, no. 6 (1975): 63–72, for one recommendation about optimal market share.

23. See Michael E. Porter, *Competitive Strategy: Techniques for Analyzing Industries and Competitors* (New York: Free Press, 1980). Part of what Porter does, to some degree in passing, is to modify the Portfolio framework in a subtle way.

24. We are indebted to our colleague, Carol K. Jacobson, for articulating this insight one summer's day on the Northrop Mall in Minneapolis.

25. For an introduction to the product life cycle idea, see Noel Capon, "Product Life Cycle," Harvard Business School Case 579-072, 1978.

26. See Arnoldo C. Hax, ed., *Readings on Strategic Management* (Cambridge, Mass.: Ballinger, 1984). For one unflattering analysis of IBM's approach to product life cycles, see Richard DeLamarter, *Big Blue: IBM's Use and Abuse of Power* (New York: Dodd, Mead & Company, 1986).

27. The coal example is used in H. Kurt Christiansen, Arnold C. Cooper, and Cornelius A. DeKluyver, "The Dog Business: A Reexamination," *Business Horizons* 25, no. 6 (1982): 12–18. The BCG matrix can be extended to indicate how competitors' positions have moved over a period of years. Strategic Planning Associates has a separate matrix to depict "share momentum." (See Hax, *Readings on Strategic Management.*) But no such device prepares the manager for the kind of surprise OPEC gave the world.

28. There is no end to the stream of poorly attested models of the spread of technology and its obsolescence. One point remains, however: it is crucially important to know when to leap from one technology to another. Unfortunately, that requires prescience. It is, at least, possible that smaller SBUs, with less invested in a given technology, are better able to make the change at the right time.

29. Note that management decision and action are thereby reduced to a source of variation in some more fundamental flow of economic forces. In this context, Portfolio researchers share considerable kinship with their counterparts in organization theory.

30. This is most famously argued by Hayes and Abernathy, "Managing Our Way to Economic Decline."

ANNOTATED BIBLIOGRAPHY

Abell, Derek F. "Using PIMS and Portfolio Analysis in Strategic Market Planning—A Comparative Analysis," Harvard Business School Case 578-617, 1977.

Allan, Gerald B. "Note on the Boston Consulting Group Concept of Competitive Analysis and Corporate Strategy," Harvard Business School Case 175-175, 1975.

Bettis, Richard A. and William K. Hall. "The Business Portfolio Approach—Where It Falls Down in Practice," *Long Range Planning* 16 (April 1983): 95–104.

Buzzell, Robert D.; Bradley T. Gale; and Ralph G. M. Sultan. "Market Share—A Key to Profitability," *Harvard Business Review* 53, no. 1 (1975): 97–106.

Ghemewat, Pankaj. "Building Strategy on the Experience Curve." *Harvard Business Review* 63, no. 2 (1985): 143–49.

Hambrick, Donald C. "Operationalizing the Concept of Business Level Strategy in Research." *Academy of Management Review* 5 (1980): 567–75. This attempt to clarify the concepts of business level strategy is a welcome event for those who are favorably disposed to the notion of operationalizing.

Schoeffler, Sidney; Robert D. Buzzell; and Donald F. Heany. "Impact of Strategic Planning on Profit Performance." *Harvard Business Review* 52, no. 2 (1974): 137–45.

Wensley, R. "PIMS and BCG: New Horizon or False Dawn?" *Strategic Management Journal* 3 (1982): 147–58. The answer is "some of both."

Wind, Yoram, and Vijay Mahajan. "Designing Product and Business Portfolios." *Harvard Business Review*, 59, no. 1 (1981): 155–65.

Yip, George S. "Market Selection and Direction: Role of Product Portfolio Planning," Harvard Business School Case 581-107, 1981.

5 THE COMPETITIVE STRATEGY FRAMEWORK

In several articles and two recent books, Professor Michael Porter of the Harvard Business School has proposed a powerful way of understanding corporate strategy. *Competitive Strategy* and *Competitive Advantage* are on the bookshelves of thousands of managers.[1] And, at least some managers have grappled with the application of the concepts that Porter develops. While Porter's ideas have a long history in the field known as "industrial economics," in which competition is only one part of the whole picture, they have become sufficiently influential to warrant affixing Porter's name to the Competitive Strategy framework. The purpose of this chapter is to interpret and critically assess the Competitive Strategy framework. In the process, we hope to convince you that Porter's approach presents clear advantages over the two approaches considered in Chapters 3 and 4.

THE BASIC IDEA

The basic idea in the Competitive Strategy framework is that a company will be more or less successful depending on certain forces at work in the company's industry. Porter urges us to think of each industry in an economy in terms of its underlying structure. The structure of an industry, on this view, will determine appropriate conduct by firms in that industry.

81

Porter translates "conduct" into a set of key factors for success. The conduct of each firm will then yield a certain level of performance, which, in turn, may feed back into an altered industry structure. This logic of Structure-Conduct-Performance (SCP) sets the context for Porter's elaboration of how to compete in a variety of industry settings. It is a logic that Porter's approach shares with the Portfolio framework discussed in Chapter 4. With both economic approaches to strategy, the first dictum for effective managerial action is clear: *pay attention first and foremost to industry structure.*

It is important to understand that, in the Competitive Strategy scheme of things, industry influence is a two-way process. Porter clearly believes that industry structure can be a powerful determinant for Liedtke's success in moving Pennzoil into the oil industry "big leagues," as well as for Ferris's efforts to launch the Allegis concept. At the same time—although secondary to the effects of structure—Porter holds out hope that astute strategic decisions can *shape* industry structure. The efforts of McGowan at MCI provide a classic case in point. The story of Execunet is, in Competitive Strategy terms, all about a competitor rewriting the rules of industry structure. Similarly, MacPhail's deliberations about the twenty-fifth man clearly involve the potential for one decisionmaker's influence on the structure of industry competition.

It is easy to see that the earlier frameworks we have discussed also reflect the SCP notion. The Harvard Policy framework asks managers to evaluate the external environment, usually taken to mean the industry, and to plan their strategy in accordance with the environmental analysis. Most of the specific models in the Portfolio framework assume that successful performance is related to others in the industry, so much so that managers are counseled to diversify, thereby minimizing the risk of being in a single industry. In fact, the whole idea of Strategic Business Units is to divide businesses into parts that face specific kinds of industry situations, where different structural forces are present.

The Historical Roots

The roots of the Competitive Strategy framework are found in the works of Bain, Penrose, Woodward, and others in the 1950s, who were trying to explain why there seemed to be differences among industries. Most classical economic theories assumed that industry structure was simply a function of market imperfection, something to be tolerated, but which needed no detailed explanation other than "markets are imperfect in the real world." Bain and others attempted to isolate the factors that led to the industry structures observed in the world.[2] Bain focused on barriers to entry facing new firms in an industry. Penrose and Woodward focused on the role of current and new technology.[3] This research also had important implications for government antitrust policy. The SCP model remains a cornerstone in the analysis and application of antitrust action.[4] We attribute the Competitive Strategy framework to Porter, not to diminish the contributions of others, but because Porter's articulation is the most influential among managers and the most easily accessible.[5]

COMPETITIVE STRATEGY AND THE FIVE FORCES OF INDUSTRY STRUCTURE

Porter claims that there are five industry forces that shape competitive strategy. These five forces determine the structure of an industry—the rules of the game—and set the constraints within which effective strategic choices are available. To be successful in an industry, a manager must understand how these forces work in his particular case, and must understand how to position his business favorably with respect to his counterparts at other companies in the industry. More specifically, Porter proposes that the level of long-term financial returns available to a firm is a function of:

1. The strength of the forces in the industry
2. The actions taken by a firm's managers to position the firm among and against these forces.

In particular, these five forces are: (1) the relative bargaining power of buyers; (2) the relative bargaining power of suppliers; (3) the threat of new entrants; (4) the threat of substitute products; and (5) the intensity of rivalrous activity among the current competitors.[6] These forces are depicted in Figure 5–1. We now consider each in turn, drawing upon a variety of case examples, including those from Chapter 2.

Relative Power of Buyers

Not all customers are alike. Selling paper clips to AT&T is very different than selling them to authors of strategy books. Taken together, the people working at AT&T need a lot of paper clips, while we need only a few.

Figure 5–1. The Five Forces of Industry Structure.

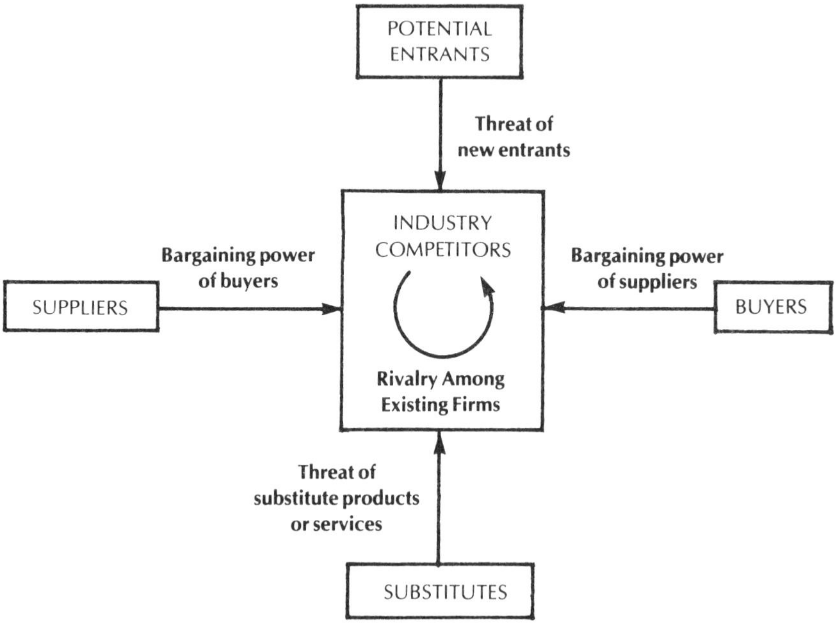
POTENTIAL ENTRANTS
Threat of new entrants
INDUSTRY COMPETITORS
Bargaining power of buyers
SUPPLIERS
Bargaining power of suppliers
BUYERS
Rivalry Among Existing Firms
Threat of substitute products or services
SUBSTITUTES

Source: Reprinted with permission of The Free Press, a Division of Macmillan, Inc. from *Competitive Strategy: Techniques for Analyzing Industries and Competitors* by Michael E. Porter, p. 4. Copyright © 1980 by The Free Press.

The price of paper clips may depend on how much of the total output of paper clips goes to large customers such as AT&T, and how much goes to small customers like us. AT&T is in a better position to negotiate among several producers for the best price, because it buys so much, while we are in no such position and really don't care to be. Relative buyer power is clearly seen here.

An industry such as metal cans is also instructive in this regard.[7] Since the packaging revolution of the 1960s, packaging materials have become increasingly integrated into the final production process. For a number of products such as beer, packaging is the key element of the product cost. As brewers, food canners, and soft drink manufacturers grew larger, and as executives turned to technologies that involved more consolidated operations, the can makers came under increased pressure. Porter would point out that the relative power of the can makers' customers had increased.

Imagine building a can manufacturing plant in St. Louis to serve Anheuser-Busch and perhaps a few others. Suppose that managers at Anheuser-Busch think that the present price is too high. The manufacturer will have little alternative but to lower the price, especially if Busch has alternative sources of supply. The manufacturer has little power vis-a-vis the customer, according to the Competitive Strategy framework; this will have a direct bearing on the operation's profitability.

The situation is radically different when selling automobiles to dealers who can be required to sell only one brand of car. The manufacturer can easily dictate prices to them, as long as they stay inside the bounds of the other forces at work in the industry.

Taking this point further, a vendor's prospects are that much greater if it can bundle a package of products for buyers who face few alternatives but to buy from it. IBM's mastery at bundling hardware and software was legend in the computer industry.[8] In a similar vein, the Allegis strategy can be understood as Ferris's attempt to increase Allegis's relative bargaining position with United customers by bundling a "travel package."

Porter claims that buyer power is high in a wide variety of circumstances.[9] Where the product represents a major cost for the buyer and/or where the buyer poses a credible threat of "backward integration," we can expect buyer power to be significant. A vivid illustration of this is telecommunications services for large corporate users. On both counts, buyer power can be significant given the development of private networks. When AT&T was slow to respond to those buyers in the early 1970s, McGowan was there with MCI's initial private-line product. According to the Competitive Strategy framework, the relative power of corporate users was an influential element of industry structure for both AT&T and MCI.

Execunet sheds new light on the importance of buyer power. According to the Competitive Strategy framework, buyer power is significant for standard—or undifferentiated—products that impose few switching costs on a buyer. Both conditions hold true for residential long-distance telephone service. Thus, McGowan was playing a very different ballgame, insofar as buyer power was concerned, as he moved MCI into the residential market.

Relative Power of Suppliers

Similarly, not all suppliers are alike. Because buying and supplying are inverse concepts, everything Porter says about buyers is applicable to the other side of the relationship. According to the framework, suppliers have more power when they have full information, earn low profits, are concentrated among a few rivals, and so on.

Again consider the plight of the can makers. If beverage canners—such as Coca-Cola—have high power as buyers, then can makers have low power as suppliers. But, the situation is actually much worse considering the identities of the suppliers of the can makers: steel and aluminum manufacturers. Traditionally, these industries have been highly concentrated, selling in multiple markets so that any one customer is relatively powerless. Indeed, in 1961 it took no less a force than the President of the United States to try to change pricing policies in the steel industry. Therefore, the can makers are relatively powerless, trapped between powerful buyers and powerful suppliers. We would expect, and Porter hypothesizes, that returns are lower than average for firms in that industry.

It is important to understand that "supply" has a very general application in the Competitive Strategy framework. Texaco's suppliers included major financial institutions. Where the act of supplying a product—here, lines of credit—begins to jeopardize the supplier, then the power of that supplier grows. The threat of a Texaco bankruptcy, coupled with the bankers' stake in a "healthy" Texaco, added to McKinley's woes. Similarly, the relative bargaining power of Allegis's major shareholders—suppliers of capital—and United pilots—suppliers of labor—severely constrained Ferris's choices.

Threat of New Entrants

One way to combat the relative power of suppliers is to threaten to enter their markets. By introducing the threat of further competition and the prospect of lower returns, a supplier that begins the process of forward (or "downstream") integration will quickly get the attention of a powerful buyer. Similarly, a buyer who begins to study the feasibility of making a product rather than buying it is more likely to get favorable terms from a powerful supplier.

The key to understanding the threat of new entrants is the concept of *entry barriers*. Entry barriers are those structural properties of an industry that prevent new competition from entering the industry and becoming successful. An entry barrier can come in many sizes and shapes and is a critical concept in understanding the Competitive Strategy framework. Porter lists seven major entry barriers: economies of scale; product differentiation; capital requirements; switching costs; access to distribution channels; cost disadvantages independent of scale; and government policy.[10]

The U.S. automobile industry clearly illustrates how these barriers can be both static and dynamic. The old saying, "What's good for General Motors is good for the U.S.A.," was true, until recently, largely because of scale. By building large plants that handled high volumes, General Motors executives were able to achieve great cost savings. The cost per automobile is less when making one million of them than when making several thousand. In order to compete with GM, companies would have to set up operations of the same order of magnitude.

An added advantage to GM was the company's ability to clearly "brand" GM products. Chevrolet, Oldsmobile, Buick, Pontiac, and Cadillac each meant something different to their die-hard customers. To the extent that GM marketers could convince consumers to be "Chevrolet families" or "Cadillac families," GM product differentiation created entry barriers for other car makers. Indeed, the very difference between GM and Ford for years lay precisely in the product differentiation strategy adopted by Pierre DuPont and Alfred Sloan in the early years of GM. GM's continued attempt at product differentiation created high switching costs, at least in the minds of consumers, and the enormity of GM operations meant that a large capital outlay was necessary to compete with them. GM had too many cost advantages, and as long as GM executives could convince the government not to bring antitrust actions against them, they had a guaranteed formula for success. The temptation for Ford and American Motors, during some good years, was always to become another GM. The Edsel and others were attempts to compete with GM when the entry barriers were, in fact, quite high. The entry barriers that emerged from GM's conduct led to an industry structure in which GM was guaranteed success. That structure, in Competitive Strategy terms, was marked by imposing deterrents to new entrants.

Threat of Substitute Products

In many cases, more than one product will perform the same function for the buyer. Airplanes can substitute for trucks, and trucks can substitute for railroads. How firms perform in an industry will be affected by the degree of substitution available to buyers of a given product.

Determining what is, and is not, a substitute product can be a tricky business. Certainly, alternative technologies can shed some insight on the matter. To see this, let's return to our example of the can industry. Caught between high buyer power and high supplier power, with both customers and suppliers threatening to enter the industry, executives at the can-making firms also face substantial pressure from substitute materials such as plastic and fiberboard. The threat of technological substitutes (e.g., plastic) reduces the flexibility of the managers in the industry to set price and service levels unilaterally.[11]

Technology does not tell the entire story here. The Competitive Strategy framework directs managers to think about the alternative ways customers could spend dollars for a given function. In technical terms from economics, "cross elasticities" among products can point to potential substitutes. MacPhail certainly must understand substitute products in this light. The Twins' spectators can, if seeking entertainment, choose from among the Twins' games, the Minnesota Zoo, local amusement parks, and so on. An understanding of substitute products hinges on an understanding of customers.

Rivalrous Activity Among the Players

The Competitive Strategy framework urges us to recognize that strategy is a matter of interdependence. On this account, the strategy for GM was successful *because* of the actions taken by executives at Ford and elsewhere. Indeed, the structure of an industry at any one point is just the sum of the actions of the participants in the industry. Strategy is dynamic rather than static, and the firm's success depends on the actions of other players. Porter puts the point succinctly: "In most industries, competitive moves by one firm have noticeable effects on its competitors and thus may incite retaliation or efforts to counter the move; that is, firms are *mutually dependent*."[12] The amount of rivalry and the degree of mutual dependence varies by industry. Some industries are routinely investigated for antitrust violations, while others are characterized by intense competition that managers internalize. Think of the rivalry between Anheuser Busch and Miller, or between Kodak and Polaroid, and compare it to the allegations of price fixing in the electrical equipment industry.[13]

Porter claims that the intensity of rivalry in an industry is a function of a number of factors, including: numerous or equally balanced competitors; slow industry growth; high fixed or storage costs; capacity augmented in large increments; lack of differentiation or switching costs; high exit barriers; high strategic stakes; and diverse competitors.[14] According to the framework then, it should come as no surprise that Ferris sought ways to distinguish United from, for example, American, Delta, and Northwest Airlines. Ferris had to contend with each of the eight rivalry factors in an industry where the product, airline passage, is rather undifferentiated.

Let's return to our example of General Motors to see how these factors work in a comprehensive story. Competition in the worldwide automobile industry has been intense during the last several years due to a change in a number of these factors. With the emergence of large, strong Japanese and European (and now Korean) companies, the number of players has increased. Customers simply have more choices. In addition, these players are diverse, representing different skills, different products, even different cultures. The myth of "buy American" is dying, making brand loyalty less a factor than it was in the 1950s. (Witness the political campaigns at work, often sponsored by companies and unions, to reinstitute this value to thereby "save American jobs.") Adding capacity in the automobile industry is not trivial. Plants take time to build and require large outlays of capital. Product and process design is not accomplished overnight, nor is capacity easily redirected. Finally, the stakes are high, as the Japanese companies have shown a remarkable ability to forgo present profitability for market presence, while Volkswagen executives make the painful decision to shut the flagship VW plant in New Stanton, Pennsylvania.

The upshot of industry rivalry should be clear. GM strategy depends on the strategies of Toyota, Nissan, Hyundai, Ford, and Volkswagen to name a few. And, similarly, Toyota's strategy depends on the strategies of these same players. It becomes a critical step in strategic analysis to understand the strategies of competitors in detail. If profits are low when rivalry is intense, strategies must be adopted to lessen the dependence on particular rivals.

Porter reminds us that yet another crucial element in understanding rivalry is signalling. Since GM's strategy depends on others' strategies, there are times when GM executives want to signal to others what they intend to do. By announcing the Saturn project as a multiyear, multibillion dollar investment, GM executives signalled Japanese companies that they did not intend to abandon the small car market to them. By announcing that IBM personal computers would be able in the future to use the UNIX operating system, IBM executives signalled to IBM customers that there was no need to switch to AT&T machines.

In sum, the move–countermove thinking that most of us associate with a good chess match or baseball game is evident in the Competitive Strategy framework. It helps us to understand the nature of dependence in an industry and the need to reassess strategic moves and signals continually.

Putting the Pieces Together with Generic Strategy

The punchline of the Competitive Strategy framework is this: *the greater the strength of industry forces, the lower the returns available to the firm.* The logic is easy to see. If a company is caught between powerful buyers and suppliers, with threats of new entrants and substitute products, and faces intense competition from current players in the industry, it will be exceedingly difficult to earn high returns. The firm's executives will have little pricing flexibility and will be unable to control supply costs. Alternatively, when these forces are not great, managers have much flexibility in price and cost control. Returns in an industry where the forces are low will be plentiful and easy to obtain.

Understanding the forces at work in an industry implies that strategy can be shaped around those forces, in order to mitigate their effects or to change them. Porter suggests three main strategies in *Competitive Strategy* that are generic to all industries: overall cost leadership, differentiation, and focus.[15] Porter intends "focus" to pertain to either cost leadership or differentiation efforts that are confined to a specific industry segment. MCI's initial private-line business was, by this definition, an attempt at a focus strategy using cost leadership techniques. Execunet, on the other hand, represented an industry-wide cost leadership strategy.

While some firms may adopt more than one of these approaches, Porter sounds a cautious note about such attempts. For every IBM that is perceived to be unique by its customers and is the low-cost producer in some products, there are a hundred firms that are "stuck in the middle," a term that conveys an inability to decide whether to focus on a segment or to be an industry-wide player, or to emphasize cost or differentiation. Let's see how these generic strategies help defend against the forces at work in an industry by returning to the example of the automobile industry.

General Motors is the classic case of a company that adopted a differentiation strategy. While Henry Ford was busy inventing the assembly line and building Model Ts that sold for less than $600, GM offered a unique car for a variety of market segments, at a variety of price points. GM executives then reinforced the branding of these cars through promotional activity. In the 1970s Japanese companies entered the U.S. market with a cost leadership strategy and underpriced General Motors with standard models and very few options.

The battle between cost leadership and product differentiation goes on today as the major companies seek to create a "world car." Meanwhile, Mercedes-Benz, Porsche, BMW, and the like are classic examples of a focus strategy. The very idea of a "BMW for everyone" is a contradiction. Each of these manufacturers targets a specific segment of the industry and seeks to differentiate a product. A different focus strategy can be seen with the Yugoslavian car known as the Yugo. Yugo executives have chosen a specific market segment *and* tried to achieve cost leadership by introducing a no-frills car for less than $4,000.

The key idea behind generic strategy is to define goals in the context of industry forces. If the forces that shape industry structure take time to change, then effective strategic choice must be conditioned on the realities that these forces impose.

The ongoing saga of General Motors clearly illustrates the importance of understanding all the forces that shape competitive strategy in an industry. Attention to dealers and customers is vital, if only to prevent others who have greater insight from winning. Even in cases where customers have little power, the answer to slow growth or sluggish earnings cannot always be "squeeze the dealers" or "raise the prices." At the same time, managing the supplier relationships is also important, even if those suppliers have very little power, for they will be a major determinant of quality. When new entrants are on the horizon, such as the Japanese and Koreans, they must be added to the equation in a manner that illustrates how the other forces in the industry will change. Finally, external forces and pressures will ensure, in most industries, a dynamic relationship among current rivals.

The Competitive Strategy framework is often accused of giving cookbook answers to complex strategic phenomena. Such a criticism is quite unfounded. Generic strategy is just that: generic. It provides rough guidelines, not detailed blueprints. Therefore, we must analyze each component part of the firm in detailing and implementing the firm's generic strategy. Porter has much to say in this regard.

THE VALUE CHAIN AND COMPETITIVE ADVANTAGE

The concept of generic strategy is activated in the Competitive Strategy framework by means of two additional concepts: *competitive advantage* and *the value chain*. Porter believes that the concept of "competitive advantage" is the key to understanding why some firms are successful and others are not. He defines the concept in this way:

Competitive advantage grows fundamentally out of value a firm is able to create for its buyers that exceeds the firm's cost of creating it. Value is what buyers are willing to pay, and superior value stems from offering lower prices than competitors for equivalent benefits or providing unique benefits that more than offset a higher price [16]

There are only two types of competitive advantage, according to the framework: cost leadership and differentiation. Each is possible for the firm whose managers adopt a focus strategy. To portray the details of how a firm can gain a cost leadership or differentiation advantage, Porter introduces what he calls "the value chain." The value chain is a remarkably simple yet powerful idea. It is one way to interpret the composition of a company or business unit.[17] It divides a company or business unit into those discrete activities that create value, or what the customer is willing to pay. Figure 5–2 is an example of a generic value chain, where the activities of the firm are divided into the *primary activities* of getting raw materials, making, selling, and servicing products, and *support activities*

Figure 5–2.   The Value Chain in the Competitive Strategy Framework.

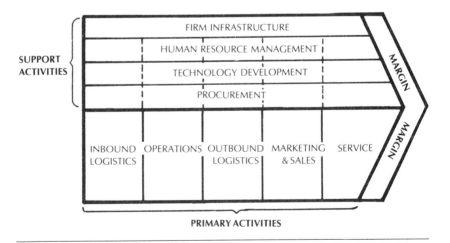

Source: Reprinted with permission of The Free Press, a Division of Macmillan, Inc. from *Competitive Advantage: Creating and Sustaining Superior Performance* by Michael E. Porter, p. 37. Copyright © 1985 by Michael E. Porter.

of purchasing, R&D, personnel, and other firm-specific activities. Each section of Figure 5–2 can be further subdivided into specific value activities. For example, marketing could be seen as a set of activities involving marketing management, advertising, sales force administration, sales force operations, providing technical literature, and promotion.[18] Lucrative margins can await those who shrewdly manage the opportunities inherent in the value chain.

Value activities do not stand alone. To really understand how the firm creates value for buyers, we must probe the linkages among value activities. Linkages exist because some value activities affect others. By understanding the linkages, we can optimize a particular activity, or coordinate the two to make each more effective. Porter urges managers to think about the value chain linkages in broad terms. In particular, he calls attention to the linkages between a firm and the firm's buyers and suppliers. Every buyer and supplier has a value chain. On this basis, Porter offers the following proposition: the more a firm understands its buyer's value chain, the greater the firm's ability to create value for that buyer. Consider, in turn, Porter's two sources of competitive advantage.

The Value Chain and Cost Advantage

A business unit obtains a cost advantage when it can perform value activities at less cost than its competitors, while creating the same value for the buyer. It becomes crucial to understand costs in a way that is consistent with Porter's whole approach, rather than in traditional accounting terms. According to the framework, a business unit must find those central costs, or *cost drivers*, that control how well the unit creates value. In Porter's terms: "Cost drivers are the structural determinants of the cost of an activity, and differ in the extent to which a firm controls them."[19]

The point is to assign assets and costs to the activities where they are important sources of value for the buyer. Different cost drivers may drive different value activities. Secondarily, the business unit must perform a competitive cost analysis. There is no other way to determine relative cost advantage.

Porter lists a number of cost drivers, including economies or diseconomies of scale, learning and spillover effects, interrelationships with other business units, and integration.[20] He goes on to argue that a cost advantage strategy can be implemented in either of two ways: (1) by directly controlling key cost drivers; and (2) by reconfiguring the firm's value chain to bring cost drivers under control. Ferris's strategic deliberations at Allegis provide simple, yet clear, cases in point.

A key asset in the travel services business, in general, is a firm's computerized reservations system. The buyer, in this instance, is the travel agent through whom corporate and pleasure travelers alike arrange their itineraries. United's Apollo system, second in volume only to American Airline's system, accounts for one-third of all airline reservations booked by travel agents.[21] Separate reservation systems have been developed for both the Hertz and Hilton components of Allegis.

According to the Competitive Strategy framework, Ferris can look first to controlling the cost drivers inherent in each of the three *separate* reservations systems. He can attend, for example, to how the information available in the Apollo system can affect travel agents' efforts to use the system promptly and accurately. Or, he can consider the most cost-effective ways of structuring the telecommunications network across which the information is provided. In this instance, economies of network scale become the relevant cost driver.

Alternatively, or additionally, Ferris could consider how cost drivers can be controlled by reconfiguring the entire Allegis value chain. This, in fact, was his oft-publicized vision for a "one-stop" travel services company.[22] Reconfiguring the value chain could mean one *integrated* reservations system for United, Hertz, and Hilton customers. This route to cost advantage, in Competitive Strategy terms, involves reworking the relationships among, at least, Firm Infrastructure (a support activity in Figure 5–2), Technology Development, and Operations (a primary activity in Figure 5–2). This reconfiguration, of course, must take travel agents' value chains into account, if cost advantage is to be a lasting achievement.

The Value Chain and Differentiation

Recall that competitive advantage through differentiation occurs, according to Porter, wherever a business unit uniquely creates buyer value at a price that the buyer is willing to pay. We tend to think of uniqueness as a property of the final product, but Porter insightfully reminds us that any value activity of the business unit can be a source of uniqueness. Product delivery systems, special marketing knowledge, and production processes are all candidates for the *uniqueness drivers* that executives can control.

Uniqueness drivers invite managers to undertake an analysis of the firm's and buyer's value chains, in similar fashion to cost driver analysis. In fact, cost drivers can be uniqueness drivers, but the focus here is not on the cost of these activities, because buyers are willing to pay higher prices for the uniqueness that these activities represent. The set of policy choices available to managers of a business unit is an important source of uniqueness. Managers can choose product attributes, the level of training and experience of personnel, levels of service, unique operations policies, and so on. The only limitations are the creativity of the managers, set against the backdrop of that which buyers will want. MacPhail's efforts to improve the Twins' playing and attendance performance is an example of the uniqueness driver concept.

First, MacPhail could think of uniqueness directly in terms of the "playing product." He could acquire the contracts of uniquely skilled pitchers, such as the knuckleballing Niekro brothers. Or he could acquire the contract of a pitcher such as Tom Seaver whose unique record of excellence could aid the Twins on the field and at the box office. Second, MacPhail could attend to such primary activities as Marketing and Sales (see Figure 5-2) to bolster attendance. One interesting uniqueness driver that Tom Peters and Nancy Austin note in *A Passion for Excellence* is the cleanliness of stadium facilities, which can attract and retain a family-oriented customer group.[23] Finally, MacPhail could reconfigure the relationship between the Twins' minor league pitching development programs (Human Resource Management or Technology Management in Figure 5–2) and specific unique pitching tactics (Operations). Several major league organizations have done precisely this by teaching all their young pitchers to throw a particular kind of pitch.[24] While this uniqueness driver may take years to bear fruitful returns, MacPhail can market the strategy as a unique point for buyer interest.

A CRITICAL ANALYSIS OF THE COMPETITIVE STRATEGY FRAMEWORK

Porter has developed a concise yet comprehensive framework for understanding the concept of strategy. On four major counts the strengths of the Competitive Strategy frameworks set it apart from the Harvard Policy and Portfolio Strategy frameworks.

First, the Competitive Strategy framework draws on a solid body of knowledge about industrial economics. It is not merely an "armchair idea" about what makes business successful. While some of the ideas are controversial, the conceptual foundations of industrial economics are accepted by many economists. By contrast, the Portfolio framework depends upon a far narrower economic idea—risk reduction—and the conceptual underpinnings of the Harvard Policy approach are unclear.

Second, the framework beautifully illustrates the old maxim, "There's nothing as practical as a good theory." Porter builds solid bridges to practice, and does so in compelling terms. In the Competitive Strategy framework, we are introduced to customers who value things as customers, suppliers who value things as suppliers, and competitors who value things as competitors. Porter, in short, provides a clearer picture of industry forces than that available in either of the other two frameworks. Buyers, for example, are harbingers of trends in the Harvard Policy approach, but nothing more concrete. Buyers disappear completely in the Portfolio Strategy story. The advantage that Porter provides is simply this: by understanding the specific forces at work in an industry, managers will be better suited to design strategies that take advantage of these forces. Managers can gain a number of insights using this framework that are not apparent if industry forces are treated as vague abstractions.

Third, the strength of the value chain idea is to focus the attention of the organization on the "basic" question: How does what we do create value for customers? The detailed focus on customers is a strength not found in the two previous frameworks. Managers must remember who generates their revenues—the customers.

Finally, the framework doesn't stop with generic strategies. It significantly improves on the earlier frameworks by giving detailed advice on how to turn generic strategies into more specific ones. After all, "build on your strengths," isn't very useful advice if accompanied by no specific plan of action that pays attention to the details of implementation. The Competitive Strategy framework establishes a standard in this regard that other competing frameworks will have to meet.

At the same time, there are some significant problems with the Competitive Strategy framework. We will examine these in the context of our three principles and case examples from Chapter 2.

A Principle About Persons

There is one overriding problem with the Competitive Strategy framework: *people are not very important in Porter's scheme of strategy*.[25] We meet no managers in the framework. Presumably—as was the case with the Portfolio Strategy framework—all people are sufficiently alike and interchangeable to warrant ignoring the Principle about Persons in a general way. Porter's gratitude to Andrews and other framers of the Harvard Policy framework, where at least some role for managers is described, makes this all the more ironic.[26]

The absence of human beings is most conspicuous in *Competitive Advantage*, a book partially about implementation. The value chain represents a ready vehicle with which Porter *could* introduce us to the everyday give-and-take between "real people" acting as buyers and suppliers. Yet, he stops short. We meet no people as buyers. They are only useful to a supplier insofar as the supplier can *extract* economic returns by knowing what buyers want and value.

We cannot understand what buyers value unless we meet them as human beings. Porter truncates that introduction. Moreover, the framework does not consider what happens when a buyer and a supplier, *both* using the framework, interact. When is a buyer's cost leadership strategy compatible with a supplier's focused search for a differentiation advantage? The value chain is too much a one-way street in this context.

A Principle of Business Basics

The Competitive Strategy framework provides a thorough analysis of certain business "basics": product quality, customer service, and competition. As noted above, Porter merits high marks for framing these issues in specific terms. At the same time, his analysis is insufficiently comprehensive in one commonplace area and is relatively vague in another. We consider each in turn.

Externalities and Business Basics. Sometimes things don't go as planned, and sometimes there are unanticipated consequences arising from one's action. The Competitive Strategy framework tends to ignore the logic of externalities. For instance, the emergence of pollution problems, or worker safety concerns, or consumer activists would be hard to identify using this framework. Business is one institution among many in society, and important linkages must be understood. One cost driver in the value chain is institutional factors, but Porter treats these almost as an afterthought.

Closely related to this point is Porter's satisfaction with treating the force of government as a secondary factor.[27] It is difficult to comprehend the problem faced by Liedtke and McKinley if we look to the Competitive Strategy framework for interpretive assistance. There is no obvious place for a Texas court judge and jury in the framework. Similarly, ignoring the role of various government officials in the entire MCI–AT&T saga is risky if we wish to understand the telecommunications industry.

Government has a pervasive influence on business and on individual firms, as do churches, universities and schools, and the family. A framework that ignores these issues may not be complete. Moreover, a framework that relies on arbitrary boundaries—as Porter does with respect to government—raises questions about its usefulness. This problem leads to our second concern with Porter's attention to business basics.

The Concept of Industry.   "Industry" is a rough concept. As Porter and others point out, the scope of an industry isn't always clear. Are railroads and trucks in the same industry? What about airlines? Automobiles? Bicycles? Tricycles? At some level of analysis, all products may be in the same industry of fulfilling human needs—not a very useful classification scheme. Therefore, the logic of industry is the logic of borderlines, as we have seen in Chapter 4, where we questioned the use of "business" in defining strategic business units. Porter does not provide a criterion for determining the scope of an industry; we are likely to be surprised by the emergence of new, unknown competitors. Watching for substitute products and new entrants is helpful only to a point: From which direction are they coming? Often, attention to industry classification is just not enough.

The second difficulty with this concept is that firms compete on a number of fronts. The Minnesota Twins compete on the playing field with the New York Yankees, at the ticket office with the Minnesota North Stars hockey team, and over the airwaves with Garrison Keillor. IBM may compete with Digital Equipment in minicomputers, but it may compete with GE or the Boy Scouts for time, attention, and the implementation of its agenda with Congress. Or, IBM may compete with McKinsey and Merrill Lynch in attracting the best university graduates. "Industry" is relevant sometimes, perhaps even most times, but not all the time.

A Principle of Timely Action

Even though our presentation of the Competitive Strategy framework is oversimplified, it conveys the feeling that managers will have to perform complex analyses. Concocting a version of the five forces that shape an industry is easy to do, but actually dividing the assets and costs of a company by value activity is quite difficult. For large Fortune 500 companies, such a process could take a long time, generate much upheaval, and perhaps tell the managers what they already know. We aren't saying that a firm shouldn't undertake such an effort, but managers ought to understand that the framework is extremely detailed and that implementation simply pervades all aspects of the firm's operations. It is difficult to go halfway with a concept like the value chain. And, it is easy to see how the Principle of Timely Action could be violated while waiting for the analysis to be completed.

CONCLUSION

Our summary judgment on the Competitive Strategy framework is that it represents an enormously useful tool for managers, and is a first-rate interpretive effort. Analytical complexities notwithstanding, the framework can be immediately useful to managers in a wide range of strategic circumstances. Moreover, the story is one with which managers can readily identify: seeking a "safe harbor" amidst a sea of inhospitable industry forces.

At the same time, the Competitive Strategy framework joins a roster of strategy frameworks that routinely ignore our Principle about Persons, or some equivalent. Implementing strategy is about change; managing a process of change is difficult. An additional body of knowledge from psychology and the humanities is directly relevant to understanding strategy as a human effort. For unknown and seemingly arbitrary reasons, Porter and others ignore that knowledge. In search of a way to link strategy with persons, we now turn to the Stakeholder Management framework of strategy.

NOTES TO CHAPTER 5

1.   There are two principal sources here: Michael E. Porter, *Competitive Strategy: Techniques for Analyzing Industries and Competitors* (New York: Free Press, 1980), and Michael E. Porter, *Competitive Advantage: Creating and Sustaining Superior Performance* (New York: Free Press, 1985). Porter has spun numerous articles from these two basic treatises.

2. See, for example, Joe S. Bain, *Industrial Organization* (New York: John Wiley & Sons, 1959), and Joe S. Bain, *Barriers to New Competition* (Cambridge, Mass.: Harvard University Press, 1956).

3. See E. T. Penrose, *The Theory of the Growth of the Firm* (Oxford: Basil Blackwell, 1959), and Joan Woodward, *Industrial Organization: Theory and Practice* (London: Oxford University Press, 1965).

4. See F. M. Scherer, *Industrial Market Structure and Economic Performance* (Boston, Mass.: Houghton Mifflin, 1980).

5. For one recent account about Porter's influence, see Walter Kiechel, IV, "New Debate about Harvard Business School," *Fortune*, November 9, 1987, pp. 34–48.

6. See Porter, *Competitive Strategy: Techniques for Analyzing Industries and Competitors*, pp. 3–29.

7. The classic case study here is "Crown Cork & Seal Company, Inc.," in C. R. Christiansen, K. R. Andrews, J. L. Bower, R. G. Hamermesh, and M. E. Porter, eds., *Business Policy: Text and Cases*, 5th ed. (Homewood, Ill.: Richard D. Irwin, 1982), pp. 112–35.

8. See Katherine Davis Fishman, *The Computer Establishment* (New York: Harper & Row, 1981) for an accessible history of the computer industry through 1980.

9. See Porter, *Competitive Strategy: Techniques for Analyzing Industries and Competitors*, pp. 113–14.

10. Ibid., pp. 7–13.

11. Ibid., pp. 23–24, 166–67.

12. Ibid., p. 17. Porter clearly understands the value of applying a game theoretic sense to strategy. See also pp. 75–87.

13. See Scherer, *Industrial Market Structure and Economic Performance*, pp. 169–71.

14. See Porter, *Competitive Strategy: Techniques for Analyzing Industries and Competitors*, pp. 17–23.

15. Ibid., pp. 34–40.

16. See Porter, *Competitive Advantage: Creating and Sustaining Superior Performance*, p. 3.

17. Porter claims that the value chain is a theory of the firm. See Porter, *Competitive Advantage: Creating and Sustaining Superior Performance*, p. 39 fn. In this regard, he clearly outdoes his Harvard Policy framework teachers.

18. Note that the value chain links information-generating activities or behaviors. Porter does not, however, seek to link the persons performing these activities. In this sense, his is a straightforward descendant of the classic model of the firm given by March and Simon, although Porter is not often considered to be an organization theorist. See James G. March and Herbert A. Simon, *Organizations* (New York: John Wiley & Sons, 1958).

19. See Porter, *Competitive Advantage: Creating and Sustaining Superior Performance*, p. 63.
20. Ibid., pp. 70–83.
21. See Agis Salpukas, "United Air Chief Gives up His Job," *New York Times*, June 26, 1987, p. 29.
22. See Kenneth Labich, "How Dick Ferris Blew It," *Fortune*, July 6, 1987, pp. 42–46. Porter might point to Ferris's apparent inability to influence the value chains of Allegis's buyers. See Porter, *Competitive Advantage: Creating and Sustaining Superior Performance,* pp. 52–53.
23. See Tom Peters and Nancy Austin, *A Passion for Excellence* (New York: Random House, 1985), p. 228. The organization they cite is the Louisville Cardinals Triple-A franchise owned by Ray Smith.
24. A notable example in recent years involves Roger Craig, manager of the San Francisco Giants and renowned master of something called the "split finger fastball."
25. According to one published report, Porter consciously distanced himself from the Harvard Policy framework emphasis on general managers and their values. See Kiechel, "New Debate about Harvard Business School," p. 48.
26. See Porter, *Competitive Strategy: Techniques for Analyzing Industries and Competitors*, p. xi.
27. Ibid., pp. 28–29.

ANNOTATED BIBLIOGRAPHY

A sampling of how industrial organization economics has been applied to strategy can be gleaned from the following:

Caves, Richard E., and Michael E. Porter. "Market Structure, Oligopoly, and the Stability of Market Shares." *Journal of Industrial Economics* 26 (1978): 285–308.
Harringan, Kathryn Rudie. *Strategic Flexibility: A Management Guide for Changing Times*. Lexington, Mass.: Lexington Books, 1985.
Rumelt, Richard P. *Strategy, Structure, and Economic Performance*. Cambridge, Mass.: Division of Research, Harvard Business School, 1974.
Teece, David J., ed., *The Competitive Challenge: Strategies for Industrial Innovation, and Renewal*. Cambridge, Mass.: Ballinger, 1987.

6 THE STAKEHOLDER MANAGEMENT FRAMEWORK

As well-known and popular as they are, the Harvard Policy, Portfolio Strategy, and Competitive Strategy Frameworks do not—taken together—close the book on the concept of strategy.[1] The purpose of Chapter 6 is to dispel such a notion.

THREE ISSUES FOR REFLECTION

We have tried thus far to convey the idea *that different stories about strategy can be told*. We have done this, in part, as a response to critics who might be tempted to conclude that the multiplicity of strategy frameworks (fact) implies a problem with the concept of strategy per se (false).[2] Each of the three frameworks discussed so far is intended to sharpen managers' understanding of strategy in different contexts. Strategy can be a complex idea. We should not be surprised then that different researchers have tried to simplify the idea in different ways; the three frameworks above are cases in point.

Second, despite evident differences in the languages and relevant contexts, *there are profound similarities across the Harvard Policy, Portfolio Strategy, and Competitive Strategy frameworks*. They share three common themes:

1. Each of the frameworks is based on an assumption that one of the tasks of strategy is to match some internal dimension of the corporation with the external environment of the corporation.
2. Each leaves the external environment largely undifferentiated. That is, actors in the environment are categorized generically, at best. Moreover, the roster of actors is a fixed set including, at most, customers, suppliers, and competitors. Government and other social/political forces are acknowledged, but are assumed to manifest themselves in the more traditional "business" or "industry" forces.
3. Across the board, it is tacitly assumed that what counts in the formulation of strategy is that which senior management designates as desirable outcomes for the firm.

The combined effect of these assumptions is to limit the context within which executives need to worry about strategy.

Third, the *justification for such limits on the relevant context of strategy becomes a crucial issue*, if those limits deny our considered understandings about the modern corporation. As we will now demonstrate, the three assumptions held in common across the Harvard, Portfolio, and Competitive Strategy frameworks are, in fact, difficult to defend. Our principle theme in this chapter is this: if the three frameworks represent the "state of the art" in relating a corporation to its environment, the concept of strategy is in trouble. One attempt to overcome these difficulties is the Stakeholder Management framework. A closer examination of the three "common" assumptions will help differentiate the Stakeholder framework.

THE MANAGERIAL MODEL OF STRATEGY

In what we call the "Managerial Model" of the corporation, the firm returns dollars to stockholders for capital, products to customers for a price, dollars to suppliers for raw materials, and jobs to employees for a pledge of loyalty. Managers are seen as the agents of stockholders who control managers via voting mechanisms and the capital market. The manager's job is to transform capital, raw material, and labor into products that customers will buy, in order to give stockholders an adequate return on their investment. "Adequate return" is defined by the available alternatives, but is always greater than the risk-free rate that an investor could obtain by buying Treasury bills.

All other activities in which the firm engages are purely instrumental. That is, they are important only insofar as they directly assist in earning returns for stockholders. This is not to say that matters of social responsibility or ethics are unimportant—both may be necessary for the creation of a good company image that helps sell products. However, they are not intrinsically important matters. According to the Managerial Model, a manager decides to act "responsibly" or not, depending on whether the action helps advance stockholders' interests.[3]

In sum, the Managerial Model depicts the corporation as a sum of instrumental processing activities—marketing, operations, finance, research, personnel, and the like—which turn out returns for stockholders. The Managerial Model is a story about preserving the *status quo* in the modern corporation.[4]

Strategy and the Managerial Model

In a number of respects, the Harvard Policy, Portfolio Strategy, and Competitive Strategy frameworks reflect the Managerial Model. Most evident are (1) the linkage between strategy and financial returns, and (2) the underlying premise that a firm is a discrete collection of process activities. But, the "Managerial" flavor is most clearly, and importantly, present insofar as the corporate status quo is concerned.

Each framework assumes that change will be piecemeal and confined to a relatively stable set of relationships among the actors in the Managerial Model. According to the model, managers need only "listen" to the signals emanating from the relationships shown in Figure 5–1. Everything else is noise, not easy to translate into decisions and corresponding actions. The Managerial Model inspires a confidence that the corporation's environment can be brought "under control" by simply declaring that to be the case.[5] So, we find Porter, for example, claiming that government policy is important, yet readily interpretable through the other forces that operate in the industry. By all appearances, Porter is simply sweeping government influence into a tidy corner. That is a bold stroke indeed.

The Managerial Model confidence extends to the links between strategy and the corporation's functional areas. If the environment can be neatly categorized, then:

1. Small changes in marketing knowledge and the normal progress of science can account for shifting customer demographics and preferences.
2. Operations management can handle the onslaught of the Japanese by introducing, for example, Kanban.

3. Finance theory marches forward from payback calculations to dis-
    counted cash flow and present value.
4. Labor relations and personnel can accommodate new ideas and de-
    velopments such as Quality Circles.

Strategy, on this view, reduces to preservation of the status quo, prin-
cipally for stockholders' interests.

The Managerial Model, however, cannot predict and cannot accommodate the emergence of new ideas, new groups, new trends, and, generally
speaking, *surprises*. It cannot process a Ralph Nader and Campaign GM,
a Foreign Corrupt Practices Act, a "60 Minutes" story, the Tylenol poison-
ings, the Rely Tampon toxic shock scare, a Judge Harold Greene, business
executives being kidnapped, the Bhopal tragedy, and a host of other
issues. By focusing their understandings of business on the traditional
relationships between customers, employees, suppliers, owners, and
domestic competitors, managers are constantly surprised by governments,
consumer advocates, environmentalists, terrorists, media, local communities, foreign competitors, and other groups who perceive that they
have a *stake* in a business.

The Managerial Model assumes that the basic rules of the game are
the same for everyone, and that the rules are relatively stable and predict-
able. *Nothing could be further from the truth in the current business
environment*. The Japanese play by one set of rules while U.S. companies
play by another and Koreans by a third. Closer to home, AT&T and IBM
play by one set of rules, while MCI and Compaq play by another. We
need a strategy framework that lets us see the shifts as ordinary. *Such a
framework must encompass business as an essentially social institution*
while continuing to observe the Principles about Persons, Business Basics,
and Timely Action. This is the context for which the Stakeholder Management framework has been developed.

THE BASIC IDEA OF STAKEHOLDER MANAGEMENT

A *stakeholder* is any individual or group who can affect, or is affected
by, actions taken by the managers of a business. The direction of stakeholder influence can be one-way or two-way, as indicated by the use of
"or" in the definition. Clearly, McGowan and deButts, as well as Liedtke
and McKinley, share two-way relationships. On the other hand, the

stinging criticisms made by a local sportswriter can make her a stakeholder for MacPhail, even if MacPhail's decisions have little or no effect on the writer's activities.[6] In this sense, the stakeholder concept allows a greater flexibility in understanding strategy problems than the frameworks already examined.

Stakes and Holders

The stakeholder concept invites managers to focus on two basic phenomena: the *stakes* that persons have in a certain action and who the *holders* of those stakes are.[7] A stakeholder relationship is forged when stakes begin to overlap in the course of strategic action. The stakeholder concept thus identifies the relevant set of actors in the environment of a business in terms of their stakes, even if we cannot neatly label that actor. In this sense, the stakeholder concept is quite general. If the actions of the Coniston partners affect Ferris, then it is that potential for affecting Ferris' stakes—such as his continued employment at Allegis—that makes the partners an Allegis stakeholder. The fact that they are stockholders does not, per se, make them key stakeholders in the Allegis saga. Rather, we must look to the specific stakes involved to identify a stakeholder relationship. Note that this emphasis on stakes differs from the Managerial Model appeal to such fixed affiliation categories as "customer," "competitor," or "stockholder."

The emphasis on *holders* requires that we match specific names and faces with the stakes in question. Although members of a group can share a stake, we must eventually move to the level of individuals to think in stakeholder terms. Thus, Liedtke cannot be satisfied with identifying a group of "Texaco suppliers" if he wants to understand the possibility of Texaco bankruptcy in stakeholder terms. Instead, he must distinguish specific bankers and their stakes from specific equipment suppliers and their stakes.

In sum, the stakeholder concept is designed to free managers from the confinement of arbitrary categories in assessing those who can affect their strategies.

Stakeholder Management

The very notion of a business takes on new meaning when stakeholders are considered. According to the Managerial Model, a business is a set of processes that eventually convert inputs into outputs for stockholders.

By contrast, a stakeholder model depicts the firm as a set, or pattern, of relationships among distinct persons holding distinct stakes of their own. The problem of *stakeholder management* thus involves maintaining a stable pattern of stakeholder relationships so that a strategy can be successfully executed. This balancing act can, by definition, take executives far afield from merely satisfying stockholders.

A Stakeholder Management framework specifies how a manager goes about balancing multiple stakeholder relationships that converge at a firm. The framework consists of three basic processes:

1. At a *rational* level of Stakeholder Management, managers must ask: How does the business as a whole fit into the larger environment?
2. At a *process* level, managers must ask: How does the business relate to the environment as a matter of standard operating procedures and routine management processes?
3. At a *transactional* level, managers must ask: How do we negotiate and execute actual deals (or contracts or understandings) with those who have a stake in our strategy?

In all three parts of the process, "environment" is translated into stakeholder terms. Obviously, these levels are connected and, in a successful business, form a coherent pattern.[8] The Stakeholder Management framework is a set of ideas, techniques, and processes designed to produce such a coherent pattern for a firm. With the aid of examples from Chapter 2, we will consider each level in turn.

STAKEHOLDER MANAGEMENT PROCESSES

Let's follow Richard Ferris through the rational level of Stakeholder Management, Andy MacPhail through the process level, and William McGowan through the transactional level. We do this merely for the sake of clearer description, since the Stakeholder Management framework points each of these executives to addressing all three levels in their own strategic contexts.

The Rational Level of Stakeholder Management

The rational level of the Stakeholder framework is designed to give an accurate picture of a business's place in the larger social environment.

At this level, managers must identify those individuals and groups who have a stake and must learn about the nature of the relationship between these stakeholders and firm. Four basic activities are involved here.

Stakeholder Identification.   Ferris must ponder several questions here, if he wants to use a stakeholder framework.

Who are those individuals and groups who can affect or are affected by the achievement of Ferris's Allegis strategy? How can Ferris construct a "stakeholder map" for Allegis? What are the problems in constructing such a map? *Ideally* the starting point for constructing a map for a particular business is an historical analysis of the environment of that particular firm. In the absence of such an historical document, Figure 6–1 can serve as a checkpoint for an *initial*, generic stakeholder map.

Figure 6–1 depicts a stakeholder map for one major strategic issue for one very large organization, the XYZ Company, based primarily in the United States. Unfortunately, most attempts at "stakeholder analysis" *end* with the construction of Figure 6–1. If he is serious about the Stakeholder Management framework, however, Ferris must move beyond generic categories of stakeholders and their stakes.

If Ferris had begun to draw a stakeholder map for Allegis early in 1987, his version of Figure 6–1 would quickly take shape. Donald Trump has accumulated a major holding of Allegis shares, although it is unclear whether his stake actually extends to taking control of Allegis. The United pilots, led by union chief F. C. Dubinsky, have offered to buy the United component of Allegis.[9] Among their stakes, job security and job seniority are clearly evident in the turbulent context of airline mergers and failures. However, Ferris must determine if the pilots' stakes are more complex than first meets the eye.

Ferris must also pencil in his Board of Directors who, in giving their tacit approval to the Allegis plan, must now be prepared for the possibility of slower profit growth while the Allegis "family" is integrated. The directors' stakes likely include the continued opportunity to sit on the Board. Yet, Ferris needs to probe whether certain key directors, such as Charles Luce, the senior Board member, are driven by other stakes.[10] In any event, their continued service on the Board is directly threatened by the Coniston partners who have publicly announced two stakes of interest to them: (1) to sit on a revamped Allegis board; and (2) to "undo" the amalgamation of United, Hertz, and Hilton.

In identifying stakeholders and their stakes, Ferris must look beyond the dispute over who controls Allegis's Board of Directors. The stakes

Figure 6–1.   Stakeholder Map of a Large Organization.

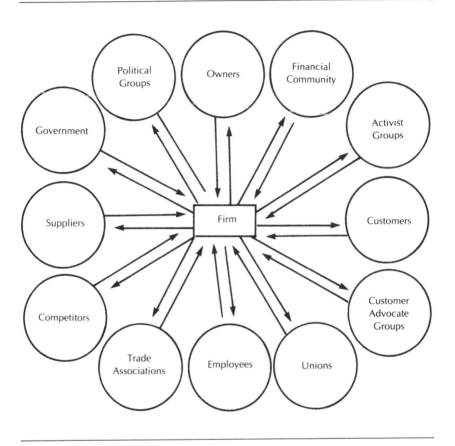

Source: From Freeman's *Strategic Management: A Stakeholder Approach,* Copyright 1984 by R. Edward Freeman, p. 55. Reprinted with permission from Ballinger Publishing Company.

of Frank Olson, chief executive at Hertz, come into play, as do the aggressive activities of Texas Air Chairman Frank Lorenzo.[11] Lorenzo would like nothing better than to taunt Ferris with selected price wars while Ferris struggles to shepherd Allegis through a shakedown period. Moreover, Ferris cannot forget Elizabeth Dole, then Secretary of the Transportation Department, who is under mounting political pressure to regulate airline performance more closely, particularly in the area of customer service. Her reputation as an effective federal bureaucrat is at stake if United operations are distracted by the Allegis start-up. Ferris, of course, can develop this oversimplified identification process further.

Stakeholder Role Sets.   Many stakeholders wear multiple hats. Managers must, in effect, understand a "stakeholder role set," those roles that an individual or group may play in the course of being a stakeholder in an organization. For example, an employee may be a customer for XYZ's products, may belong to a union at XYZ, may be an owner of XYZ, may be a member of a political party, and may even be a member of a consumer advocate group. Many members of certain stakeholder groups are also members of other stakeholder groups and, as stakeholder in an organization, may have to balance (or not balance) conflicting and competing roles. Conflict within each person and among group members may result. The role set of a particular stakeholder may well generate different and conflicting expectations of corporate action.

At the rational level of stakeholder analysis, Ferris must look beyond the mere enumeration of stakeholders to comprehend the role set idea. The United pilots are owners and employees. What is attractive to them as owners may seriously harm their stakes as employees, and vice versa. Olson is both an employee and a potential rival to Ferris for the CEO's chair. Ferris cannot be satisfied with a simple and cursory assessment of each stakeholder's stakes. Sometimes, as when role sets enter the picture, those stakes need to be understood as *each stakeholder would prioritize them*.

Stakeholder Networks and Coalitions.   Stakeholders do not act in isolation, nor do they only interact with the firm. The Stakeholder Management framework points out that stakeholders are enmeshed in patterns of relationships of their own. This phenomenon heightens the intrigue surrounding why certain stakeholders choose to hold the stakes that they do and, accordingly, act as they do.[12]

Ferris confronts this issue with Dubinsky and the Coniston partners. Amidst his efforts to have the Allegis directors take the pilots' takeover offer seriously, Dubinsky announced that he would consider joining forces with Coniston, if necessary. The Coniston partners admitted that they had met with the pilots' representatives and, moreover, that they would find a role for the pilots in any Coniston-led coup at Allegis.[13] In pondering the effects of his actions on the stakes of the pilots, Ferris must recognize that the pilot-Coniston coalition complicates his available range of actions. The pattern of coalitions can, of course, be far more intricate than this.

Multiple Dimensions of Stakeholders' Stakes.   Stakeholders also have different outlets available to them for advancing and protecting their stakes. Think of these outlets as being available in different flavors, or kinds of power. By matching different kinds of stakes with different kinds of outlets, we can use the Stakeholder Management framework to sharpen our understanding of stakeholders' agendas.

One way to capture the multiple dimension problem is to draw a two-dimensional scheme that pairs stakes with sources of stakeholder power. Although there are no hard and fast criteria to apply here, one can classify stakes in a range from "having an equity interest in the firm" to "being an influencer." Influencers—or kibitzers—have an interest in what the firm does because it affects them in some way, even if not directly in marketplace terms.[14] We might place a middle category between equity and influencer and call it a "market" stake. These three categories of a continuum are meant to represent the more traditional theory of the firm's differing stakes held by owners (equity stake), customers and suppliers (market stake), and government (kibitzer).

The second dimension of this scheme can be understood in terms of power, or loosely speaking, the ability to use resources to make an event actually happen. The three points of interest on this continuum are voting power, economic power, and political power. Owners can expend resources in terms of voting power, by voting for directors or voting to support management, or even "voting" their shares in the marketplace in a takeover battle. Customers and suppliers can expend resources in terms of economic power, measured by dollars invested in R&D, switching to another firm, raising price, or withholding supply. Government agents can expend resources in terms of political power by passing legislation, writing new regulations, or bringing suit in the courts. The two-dimensional scheme is shown in Figure 6–2.

The diagonal of Figure 6–2 represents the development of classical management thought and the prevailing world view of the modern business firm, a view that we have labeled the Managerial Model. Management concepts and principles have evolved to treat the firm's stakeholders along this diagonal. Managers learn how to handle stockholders and boards of directors via their ability to vote on certain key decisions. Conflicts with equity stakeholders are resolved by the procedures and processes written into the corporate charter or by methods involving formal legal parameters. When dealing with "economic" stakeholders, strategic planners, marketing managers, financial analysts, and operations executives base their decisions on marketplace variables and a long tradition of wisdom and

Figure 6–2.   Multiple Dimensions of Stakeholders' Stakes.

POWER STAKE	Formal or Voting	Economic	Political
Equity	Stockholders Directors Minority Interests		
Economic		Customers Competitors Suppliers Debt Holders Unions	Foreign Governments
Influencers			Consumer Advocates Government Nader's Raiders Sierra Club Trade Association

Source: From Freeman's *Strategic Management: A Stakeholder Approach,* Copyright 1984 by R. Edward Freeman, p. 63. Reprinted with permission from Ballinger Publishing Company.

research based on an economic analysis of marketplace forces. When dealing with "influence" stakeholders, public relations and public affairs managers and lobbyists learn to deal in the political arena, to curry the favor of politicians and to learn to use political action committees (PACs) and the regulatory process strategically.

Increasingly, the business environment cannot be neatly summarized along, and confined to, the diagonal of Figure 6–2. The multidimensional scheme is designed to call attention to the "off diagonal" contexts that can seriously affect a company's strategies.

For instance, in the auto industry one part of government—the Chrysler Loan Guarantee Board—acquired formal power, while in the steel industry, some agencies have acquired economic power through the imposition of import quotas or the trigger-price mechanism. The SEC might be viewed as a kibitzer with formal power over disclosure and accounting rules. Outside directors do not necessarily have an equity stake. This is especially true of women, minority group members, and academics whose presence on the boards of large corporations is now normal. Some traditional kibitzer groups are buying stock and acquiring an equity stake; while they also acquire formal power, their yearly demonstration at the stockholders meeting, or the proxy fight over social issues, is built upon their political power base. Witness the marshalling of the political process by church groups in bringing up issues such as selling infant formula in the Third World or investing in South Africa. Unions are using political power as well as their equity stake, in terms of pension fund investing, to influence management decisions. Ferris clearly understands this general "off diagonal" phenomenon with regard to the United pilots.

The upshot is that the rational level of Stakeholder Management involves understanding not only stakeholders and their stakes, but also the means available to them for advancing their stakes. This makes Ferris's identification activities all the more complicated. At the same time, it suggests that stakeholder identification is only the tip of the iceberg. In order to guide managers toward meeting stakeholders on various turfs, the rational level of analysis must be tempered by a thorough understanding of the workings of an organization. This understanding must be developed through an analysis of strategic and operational processes there. This *process level*, then, addresses how well managers are prepared to deal with stakeholders once they have been identified.

THE PROCESS LEVEL OF STAKEHOLDER MANAGEMENT

Large complex organizations and small partnerships alike have many processes for accomplishing tasks. From routine applications of procedures and policies to the use of more sophisticated analytical tools, managers invent processes to accomplish routine tasks and to make complex tasks routine. Organizational processes serve multiple purposes. One well-known purpose is to facilitate communication about those norms for which the corporation stands, which are specific reflections of "how we do things around here." If managers understand these norms, the story goes, they can design the process activities necessary for success in the organization.

The Stakeholder Management framework builds on this theme about organizational processes. In this view, the activities necessary for success "inside" the organization must bear some relationship to the tasks that the "outside" environment requires of the organization's managers, if the organization is to be a successful and ongoing concern. Therefore, if the external environment is a rich multistakeholder one, the strategic processes of the organization must reflect this complexity. These processes need not be baroque, multistep, rigid analytical devices. Rather, existing strategic processes that work reasonably well can be enriched with a concern for multiple stakeholders. The point of the process level of stakeholder management follows accordingly: *in order to manage stakeholder relationships, your organizational processes must "smell" of stakeholders throughout.*[15]

The process level of stakeholder management emphasizes adapting existing strategic planning processes so that the *correct questions about the rational level* are routinely asked. In other words, the language of strategic planning can be more useful if talk about stakeholders is part of talk about missions, programs, budgets, and control. One example of adapting a planning process is shown in Figure 6–3. Note that a question about stakeholders is raised at every turn. Let's consider how MacPhail might apply the process idea.

Suppose that MacPhail decides that his problem with the Twins pitching staff can be alleviated by the addition of a twenty-fifth man on the team roster. In considering that direction, he is guided by the Stakeholder Management framework to ask certain questions *at the very outset* of his deliberations.[16] His identification of such stakeholders as his Board of Directors, his on-the-field manager, his counterparts at other teams, and the local sportswriters, leads him to ponder how those persons will affect his strategic program. These considerations, in turn, compel MacPhail to determine where he might need to devote resources to deal with these stakeholders. For example, the addition of the extra player will probably subject MacPhail and the Twins to added media attention. Resources—human and financial—will be needed to respond. Also, a CEO at another team may decide to engage MacPhail in a "bidding war" over candidates for the twenty-fifth spot. This will require added financial resources. All these considerations lead, in turn, to MacPhail's need for a frame of reference to assess the worth of his decision. By asking "What does stakeholder X want?", MacPhail can assess whether his strategy is on track relative to that stakeholder. The punch line for the process level is simply this: if managers routinely have to answer questions about their stakeholders, they will likely pay attention to managing stakeholder relationships.

Figure 6–3. The Strategic Planning Process and Stakeholder Management.

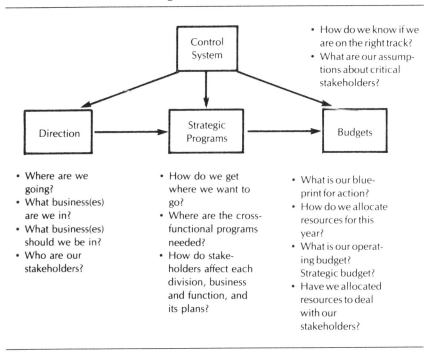

Source: From Freeman's *Strategic Management: A Stakeholder Approach,* Copyright 1984 by R. Edward Freeman, p. 69. Reprinted with permission from Ballinger Publishing Company.

THE TRANSACTIONAL LEVEL OF STAKEHOLDER MANAGEMENT

The culminating step in Stakeholder Management is the negotiation and execution of a set of transactions that satisfy the firm and the firm's stakeholders. According to this framework, all the rational- and process-level activities in the world will be futile if not carried to fruition as lasting transactions with stakeholders. At the same time, the absence of careful attention to identifying and incorporating stakeholder concerns into strategic planning is a sure recipe for failed attempts at stakeholder transactions. The three levels of Stakeholder Management are thus vitally linked.

We expect that managers will find the notion of stakeholder transactions to be both familiar and threatening. On the first count, many managers see themselves as deal makers.[17] Transactions are very commonplace and familiar to them. They engage in everyday exchanges with such stakeholders as customers, suppliers, stockholders, union representatives, and members of the media, and find the entire matter quite natural. Yet when compelled to move from this relatively comfortable zone of transactions to deal with the changes that have occurred with traditional marketplace stakeholders, and with the emergence of new stakeholder groups, many managers are understandably uncertain. The Stakeholder Management framework diverges sharply from the Managerial Model here by proposing that these newer, tougher stakeholder transactions are no less important than the traditional set of everyday business transactions. More disconcerting still, the Stakeholder approach implies that stakeholder concerns are, all else equal, *legitimate* concerns.[18] This notion challenges the Managerial view that it is up to a manager alone to determine what is, or is not, a legitimate influence on his business.

Transactions with stakeholders can take many forms. Direct contact with stakeholders, in ongoing dialogues, is a preferred route in the Stakeholder framework. Where that avenue is not available—as in the case of transacting with competitors in contexts of antitrust concern—more subtle, tacit transactions are options. Regardless of the means employed, the Stakeholder Management framework holds this dictum for managers: *the more voluntarily companies enter into stakeholder transactions, the more likely they can create mutually beneficial stakeholder relations.*[19] MCI's McGowan provides a classic case in point.

MCI and Stakeholder Transactions.   McGowan has been portrayed in print as an executive who sees management in terms of a web of "businesses," which amount, in fact, to deals that stabilize ongoing relationships.[20] One important and celebrated stakeholder transaction involved McGowan and various officials at the Federal Communications Commission.[21] McGowan clearly had a stake in the rules emanating from the FCC regarding competition in the telecommunications marketplace in the early 1970s. Just as clearly, FCC officials had a stake in McGowan's fledgling company, since MCI's success could serve as patent evidence that competitors could operate alongside AT&T. McGowan voluntarily entered into an ongoing dialogue with FCC officials about MCI's experiences and problems with AT&T. Even when, late in the Execunet saga, FCC officials took an adversarial stance regarding McGowan, his transactional experiences enabled him to choose how to respond intelligently.

McGowan also entered into a series of transactions with MCI's financiers.[22] In order to make clear MCI's plight—before Execunet—and thus calm nervous bankers, McGowan included their representatives in MCI strategy discussions. And, when certain of these supplier stakeholders began to squirm at MCI's financial woes, McGowan voluntarily sought to rearrange these stakeholder transactions for everyone's gain.[23]

McGowan even transacted with his arch stakeholder, AT&T's John deButts. Part of the transaction was direct; McGowan met with deButts on at least one occasion and with other AT&T officials more often.[24] But, just as important, he pursued a pattern of action that sent clear signals, a form of tacit transaction, to deButts that he, McGowan, was not going to disappear.[25] This, coupled with McGowan's more explicit transactional efforts, had the effect of preserving a sphere, albeit a shaky one, in which MCI was able to grow slowly.

Successful transactions with stakeholders are built on understanding the legitimacy of stakeholders and using processes to surface their concerns routinely. However, as McGowan's efforts reveal, the transactions themselves must be executed by managers who understand the "currencies" in which the stakeholders seek to be "paid." According to the framework, there is simply no substitute for thinking through how a particular individual can benefit *and* how the organization can benefit at the same time. Anything less is bound to fail as a stakeholder transaction.

A CRITICAL ANALYSIS OF THE STAKEHOLDER MANAGEMENT FRAMEWORK

The Stakeholder Management framework differs significantly from the Harvard Policy, Portfolio Strategy, and Competitive Strategy frameworks on a very basic issue: how to interpret the modern corporation. From the Stakeholder perspective, the corporation is a social institution whose walls are permeable by a host of persons and groups with a stake in corporate action. From the Managerial perspective that underlies the other three frameworks, the corporation is an institution that is meaningfully separable from (that is, different in kind) other social institutions such as government, family, and schools. The distinction can be carried further. From the Stakeholder vantage point, the corporation is a fragile institution, continually subject to revision as stakeholders come and go. Accordingly, strategy is an uncertain, dynamic process of juggling diverse and conflicting stakeholder relationships that make up the corporation. By contrast, the corporation is a stable institution, according to the other three frameworks, and strategy is an analytical exercise in positioning the firm against an environment which, although changing, is also inherently stable.

Now, one way to assess the Stakeholder Management framework critically is to subject it to an empirical test of whether the framework "accurately" describes the modern business world. However, such a test will likely raise more questions than it solves for two reasons. First, as we discussed early in Chapter 6, how managers think of strategy is largely a matter of how they choose to tell their stories—that is, how they specify the contexts in which they are interested.[26] The Stakeholder Management framework adds another dimension to the stories told in Chapters 3, 4 and 5. Second, and precisely because the Stakeholder framework tells another story, a "reality" test is meaningless. We have, in fact, shown throughout this chapter that the business world can be interpreted in stakeholder terms.

There is another way to assess the Stakeholder Management framework critically and compare it to the three other frameworks that, at one level, seem so different from the Stakeholder notion. That way, once again, is provided by the three principles in our logic for strategy. We will now show that the Stakeholder Management framework has definite strengths and one important weakness.

A Principle About Persons

Individual persons, holding and directed by their own stakes, are the cornerstones of the Stakeholder framework. The framework guides managers to put names and faces to those persons who affect, or are affected by, managers' strategic activities. Accordingly, the Stakeholder Management framework provides the clearest demonstration thus far in this book of how a strategy framework can take rich account of individual persons.

The only cause for equivocation on this point is the fact that stakeholders can be individuals *or* groups. This presents a potential problem inasmuch as the whole Stakeholder point is to get away from treating persons—for strategic purposes—as generic entities. As long as managers recognize that a group can be usefully considered a stakeholder *only* as long as each member of the group has similar stakes, then the practice of group identification remains consistent with the framework. More often than not, because members of a group come and go, managers will still need to probe beyond "group" to the individual members.

A Principle of Business Basics

The Stakeholder Management framework provides the most extensive coverage of business basics, when compared to the Harvard, Portfolio, and Competitive Strategy frameworks. This should come as little surprise. Because the framework presupposes that the business firm is a social institution populated by any individual or group whose stakes are affected, "stakeholder" and "business basics" become virtually synonymous. Put somewhat differently, any of the business basics in our principle can be understood as a stakeholder relationship. This extensive coverage is the source of both a significant benefit for, and a potential cost imposed upon, managers.

Stakeholder Management and Business Ethics. The Stakeholder framework provides a context within which managers can see and act upon the connections between business—more particularly, strategy— and ethics.[27] If managers decide to see business as a network of stakeholder relationships, then they can more clearly understand the connection between business and ethics.

Often managers and business commentators react to the phrase "business ethics" as if the term represents a contradiction. But "ethics" is not a mysterious word. To call an issue "an ethical issue" is merely to single it out as having to do with who is harmed or benefited by the issue.[28] Accordingly, *most business issues are ethical issues.* Ethics is concerned with how various agents, individuals or groups, interact on important matters. It deals with the distribution of benefits and burdens, rights and duties, and provides more fundamental reasons for the decisions that managers make.

Because the usual way that we talk about business—in terms of technology, markets, profits, capital, etc.—does not always call for the identification of specific agents involved in a business decision, the ethical nature of business is often obscured. The Stakeholder framework and language are a better way to talk about business, because they clearly show us that many business decisions concern a number of parties (stakeholders), each of whom is harmed or benefited to some degree.[29]

The Stakeholder Management framework thus *sets the stage* for analyzing the ethical aspects of strategic actions. The link between strategy and ethics is most vivid at the transactional level of Stakeholder Management. Here, individuals meet other individuals, as stakeholders, in a face-to-face attempt to work out one of the most fundamental questions of ethics:

How should we treat our fellow human beings? It is simply not possible to get to this point in the analysis by using any of the other three strategy frameworks.

Stakeholder Management and the Limits of Managerial Comprehension. The very generality of the Stakeholder framework poses a potential problem for managers. Because the framework provides no neat boundaries separating "business basics" from "business trivia," and because the Stakeholder approach implies a proactive stance, managers can easily feel overwhelmed. This problem can take one of two forms. First, the central "business basics" can become crowded out of the manager's agenda. The time that McGowan had to devote to regulatory stakeholders surely diverted his attention from customers. Second, a manager may try to engage in projects in which he has little or no expertise. Liedtke's forte is running an oil company. Dealing with stakeholders such as Wall Street lawyers and Texas judges is a different issue.

Nothing in the Stakeholder Management approach mandates that managers ignore the business basics of product quality, customer service, and competition. Yet, the potential exists for violation of our Principle of Timely Action.

A Principle of Timely Action

The Stakeholder Management framework will probably not satisfy those looking for a simple, prepackaged formula for understanding a firm's environment. The framework translates a basic assumption about environmental complexity into a detailed analysis of many, interrelated stakeholder relationships. The framework will probably further disappoint those searching for a set of off-the-shelf rules that can be applied to stakeholder transactions.[30] Stakeholder Management, instead, places a premium on the art of decisionmaking. The Stakeholder approach is designed to lead managers to the point of decision, but not to *the* answers per se.

On both counts, then, the Stakeholder framework bears the seeds of "analysis paralysis." Timely action could be inhibited as a result. One way out of this trap is for managers to understand that the analysis of stakeholder relationships (that is, the rational level) is merely the beginning of the Stakeholder Management process. The framework thus leaves it up to managers to focus on stakeholder transactions as the culminating effort. This holds until, of course, the stakeholder map needs to be redrawn.

CONCLUSION

A very different, and quite comprehensive, view of corporations and strategy is available to those who choose to employ the Stakeholder Management framework. The framework clearly outdistances the Harvard Policy, Portfolio Strategy, and Competitive Strategy frameworks when all four are compared on our Principle about Persons and Principle of Business Basics. However, a satisfactory approach to our Principle of Timely Action still eludes us. Perhaps closer attention to process, as suggested by the Stakeholder framework, is the answer. With that possibility in mind, we now complete our assessment by turning to two process approaches to strategy.

NOTES TO CHAPTER 6

1. This observation might come as a surprise, if your reading of the strategy research literature were confined to the *Strategic Management Journal.*
2. For a gloomy research survey that reflects, in part, this theme, see Colin Camerer, "Redirecting Research in Business Policy and Strategy," *Strategic Management Journal* 6, no. 1 (1985): 1–15.

   This is not to say that multiplicity per se is a valuable commodity. That particular position is apparently taken in James Brian Quinn, Henry Mintzberg, and Robert M. James, *The Strategy Process* (Englewood Cliffs, N.J.: Prentice-Hall, 1988), pp. 1–2.

   In contrast to these two positions, our point is that multiplicity is an irrelevant indicator of whether the concept of strategy is worthwhile. Rather, our three principles point to a test of the *usefulness* of any particular model in a managerial context. A strategy model that cannot help a manager understand her trials and tribulations is pointless.
3. This point is patently clear in Kenneth Andrews, *The Concept of Corporate Strategy*, revised ed. (Homewood, Ill.: Richard D. Irwin, 1980). That this is only one conception of corporate responsibility comes as news to many strategy researchers. For a more expansive treatment, see R. Edward Freeman and Daniel R. Gilbert, Jr., *Corporate Strategy and the Search for Ethics* (Englewood Cliffs, N.J.: Prentice-Hall, 1988).
4. A vivid illustration of this is visible in Oliver Williamson's conception of corporate governance. See Oliver E. Williamson, *The Economic Institutions of Capitalism* (New York: Free Press, 1985), pp. 298–325.

   For a critical review of this concept, see R. Edward Freeman, "The Economic Institutions of Capitalism, Oliver Williamson," *Academy of Management Review* 12, no. 2 (1987): 385–87.

5. The exemplar here is, of course, the Harvard Policy framework. We wonder what strategy research would look like today if the Harvard Policy framers had rallied around the arguments of Thomas Schelling, rather than Alfred Chandler and Chester Barnard. One manifestation of this control imagery is the notion of "crisis management." See Clare Ansberry, "Oil Spill in the Midwest Provides Case Study in Crisis Management," *Wall Street Journal*, January 8, 1988, p. 21.

6. For an introductory discussion about stakeholders, see R. Edward Freeman, *Strategic Management: A Stakeholder Approach* (Boston: Ballinger, 1984), pp. 43–47.

7. Gilbert argues that such an emphasis upon *nouns* sets the stakeholder model apart from the rest of the strategy field, where the key concepts are *verbs*. See Daniel R. Gilbert, Jr., "Strategy and Justice" (Ph.D. diss., University of Minnesota, 1987), chap. 5.

8. The "pattern" imagery is deliberately chosen. See Freeman, *Strategic Management: A Stakeholder Approach*, p. 110.

9. See, for example, Judith Valente and Scott Kilman, "Pilots May Seek Partner to Buy Parent of United," *Wall Street Journal*, April 27, 1987, p. 6.

10. See Peter Finch, "You Call This Retirement?" *Business Week*, June 29, 1987, p. 30.

11. See Jeff Bailey and Laura Landro, "Olson Navigates in Turbulence at Allegis," *Wall Street Journal*, June 11, 1987, p. 28.

12. See Freeman, *Strategic Management: A Stakeholder Approach*, pp. 54–64.

13. See Valente and Kilman, "Pilots May Seek Partner to Buy Parent of United," and Laurie P. Cohen and Judith Valente, "Coniston to Seek Control of Allegis Board, Says It Would Sell All or Part of Concern," *Wall Street Journal*, May 27, 1987, pp. 3, 23.

14. See William Dill, "Public Participation in Corporate Planning: Strategic Management in a Kibitzer's World," *Long Range Planning* 8, no. 1 (1975): 57–63.

15. The "smell" imagery is taken from Tom Peters and Nancy Austin, *A Passion for Excellence* (New York: Random House, 1985), pp. 107–11.

16. In other words, concerns with implementation accompany—rather than follow—concerns with formulation.

17. This point is well-documented in the business press, even if it has escaped notice in the strategy research literature. You can capture the deal-making flavor in Larry Kahaner's quasi-biography of MCI Chairman William McGowan. See Larry Kahaner, *On the Line: The Men of MCI—Who Took on AT&T, Risked Everything, and Won!* (New York: Warner Books, 1986).

   The latest in the deal-making genre is Donald Trump's own story. See Donald Trump, with Tony Schwartz, *Trump: The Art of the Deal* (New York: Random House, 1987).

   We are indebted to Donald J. Herman at NCR Comten and NCR for his lessons in the art of deal-making.

18. See Freeman, *Strategic Management: A Stakeholder Approach*, pp. 22–24.
19. Ibid., pp. 74–80. A disposition to engage stakeholders voluntarily is a premise that permeates Freeman's Stakeholder Management Capability concept.
20. See Kahaner, *On the Line: The Men of MCI—Who Took on AT&T, Risked Everything, and Won!*.
21. See Steve Coll, *The Deal of the Century: The Break Up of AT&T* (New York: Atheneum, 1986), pp. 45–52.
22. See Kahaner, *On the Line: The Men of MCI—Who Took on AT&T, Risked Everything, and Won!*, pp. 113–16.
23. Ibid., pp. 142–43.
24. See Coll, *The Deal of the Century: The Break Up of AT&T*, pp. 21–27.
25. See Gilbert, "Strategy and Justice," regarding how tacit transactions, known as "conventions," can provide insights into strategic interaction.
26. That managers have a choice of the stories they can tell is a principal theme in Freeman and Gilbert, *Corporate Strategy and the Search for Ethics*.
27. Ibid.
28. Ibid., chap. 3.
29. Schelling's conception of strategy guides us here. See Thomas C. Schelling, *The Strategy of Conflict* (Cambridge, Mass.: Harvard University Press, 1960).
30. See Freeman and Gilbert, *Corporate Strategy and the Search for Ethics*, chap. 4 as an attempt to extend the stakeholder framework in this way. The vehicle there is the concept of enterprise strategy. See also Freeman, *Strategic Management: A Stakeholder Approach*, pp. 89–110.

ANNOTATED BIBLIOGRAPHY

The Stakeholder Management framework is an adaptation of ideas expressed in the following diverse set of arguments:

Allison, Graham T. *Essence of Decision*. Boston, Mass.: Little, Brown, 1971.
Berle, Adolf A., and Gardiner C. Means. *The Modern Corporation and Private Property*. New York: Commerce Clearing House, 1932.
Brams, Steven J. *Biblical Games*. Cambridge, Mass.: MIT Press, 1981.
Evan, William. *Organization Theory: Structures, Systems, and Environments*. New York: John Wiley & Sons, 1976.
Evan, William, ed. *Interorganizational Relations*. Philadelphia: University of Pennsylvania Press, 1976.
Hirschman, Albert O. *Exit, Voice and Loyalty*. Cambridge, Mass.: Harvard University Press, 1970.
McDonald, John. *The Game of Business*. New York: Anchor Press, 1977.

Muzzio, Douglas. *Watergate Games: Strategies, Choices, Outcomes*. New York: New York University Press, 1982.

Rawls, John. *A Theory of Justice*. Cambridge, Mass.: Harvard University Press, 1971.

Sonnenfeld, Jeffrey. *Corporate Views of the Public Interest*. Boston, Mass.: Auburn House, 1981.

Thompson, James D. *Organizations in Action*. New York: McGraw-Hill, 1967.

7 THE PLANNING PROCESS FRAMEWORK

The Stakeholder Management framework places the concept of strategy in a context far more complex than those of the Harvard Policy, Portfolio Strategy, and Competitive Strategy frameworks. We can see this complexity in two primary forms. First, the Stakeholder framework provides managers with both a general picture of business basics *and* a requirement that specific names and faces be attached to these basics. Managers using the framework cannot make a simple trade-off between scope and detail, as tempting as that might be. Second, the Stakeholder framework emphasizes that a strategy is not complete until specific stakeholder transactions, explicit or tacit, are in place. Strategy, from the Stakeholder perspective, is not something managers do *to* their environments. Rather, strategy is executed *with* other persons who make up that environment.

All this poses a potential problem with our Principle of Timely Action (see Chapter 1). Complex strategic analysis begs for efficient techniques, lest strategy becomes an exercise in paralysis and hence futility. This suggests that *how* strategies are put together might play an important part in giving managers the tools for timely action.[1] A host of strategy models have, in fact, been developed around the notion that it matters greatly how strategic plans are shaped. This notion about strategy will be the subject of this chapter and Chapter 8.

STRATEGIC PLANNING, STRATEGY, AND PLANNING PROCESS

To many managers and researchers, strategic planning, planning process, and strategy are interchangeable concepts. Indeed, as we observed in Chapter 1, a widely held concept of strategy reflects this very point. Strategy is widely believed to be a set of important decisions derived from systematic decisionmaking procedures.[2]

As widespread as this notion is, we believe that it represents just one possible concept of strategy. Beginning in Chapter 1, we have been building the case that *strategy* applies in a variety of contexts and frameworks, some of which have nothing to do with the procedures for planning a strategy. Thus, our attention here is directed toward one subset of strategy frameworks that advises managers how to do strategic planning. Since the emphasis is placed on process, or procedural, matters, we call this the *Planning Process framework*.[3] In Chapter 8, we will consider an extension of this framework known as the Seven-S framework.

The Basic Idea

The main idea of the Planning Process framework is simply this: the most important aspect of strategy is the way decisions are made and implemented. Planning is hardly a new technique or concept. We can understand the Greek generals, prehistoric mammoth hunters, medieval traders and artisans, and eighteenth century industrialists alike in terms of their efforts to prepare for an uncertain future in some deliberate way. What is modern about all this is the formalization of processes for business planning and the articulation of step-by-step procedures for developing corporate, divisional, and business unit strategic plans.

The mark of effective strategists, according to the logic of the Planning Process framework, is how well they devise and carry out procedures for fitting their firms with the environment.[4] Managers using such a framework thus need to keep one basic proposition in mind: the more closely a specific decisionmaking procedure is followed, the better the strategy will be.[5] This emphasis upon procedure is firmly rooted in two basic assumptions that managers must make about themselves: (1) managers have limited reasoning capabilities; and (2) managers do not always opt for the "best" way to act. If not for these assumptions, there would simply be no point for following the Planning Process framework.[6]

THE BASIC PROBLEM FOR MANAGERS

William McGowan, Hugh Liedtke, Richard Ferris, and Andy MacPhail each has a problem, according to the Planning Process framework: each takes shortcuts when it comes to processing information about the strategic problem he faces. Two particular kinds of shortcuts can affect strategic planning in a major way.

First, none of these men considers all the possible alternative solutions to his problem and none gathers all the information about all the alternatives. Instead, each limits his analysis to only those strategic alternatives that are practical and feasible and about which it is feasible to gather appropriate data. McGowan considers other kinds of domestic long-distance service, but not trans-Atlantic data communications, in 1974. Liedtke ponders various settlements with McKinley, but apparently not a third-party "friendly" buyout of Texaco. Ferris collects a rental-car company and a hotel company, but not a passenger train company. MacPhail scans a list of recently unemployed pitchers, but does not consider different ways of redefining the job descriptions for his current pitching staff. These executives limit the strategic options available for their organizations simply because they are unable, as human beings, to process very much information. This condition has been labelled "bounded rationality" by Nobel laureate Herbert Simon.[7] Yet, the problem for managers goes deeper still when it comes to strategic planning.

McGowan, Liedtke, Ferris, and MacPhail compound the matter by taking a second shortcut. From an already limited set of alternatives—the bounded rationality result—each man is prone to accept the first convenient and satisfactory solution available to him. Rather than calculate whether Execunet provides a return on investment of 15 percent for 1976–1980, McGowan decides to pursue Execunet because it will help stave off MCI's creditors. Rather than calculate the optimal settlement terms under different scenarios, Liedtke pegs a settlement figure in order to grab McKinley's attention. Rather than study the optimal pattern of customer flows among different air carriers and rental-car companies at American airports, Ferris decides to buy Hertz intact. Rather than track down every relief pitcher who has been unemployed since 1982, MacPhail employs the services of one pitcher after another who appears able to provide immediate assistance for the Twins. These executives further limit the strategic options for their companies by settling on a comfortable, but not optimal, course of action. Simon has called this tendency "satisficing."[8] Satisficing behavior compounds the consequences of bounded rationality, according to the Planning Process framework.

These observations certainly seem routine enough. They may, in fact, seem laughable or trivial. Certainly, we can only deal with so much information before we feel overwhelmed. Certainly, too, we often must decide to act when we cannot afford to wait for an optimal calculation. (We have chosen boundedly, and satisficed, in presenting only six frameworks, rather than twenty here.) There is nothing remarkable, at first glance, about bounded rationality and satisficing behavior.[9] We, as persons, can only work with the reasoning capabilities dealt our way.

"Not so," say the Planning Process framers. Bounded rationality and satisficing behavior are major problems for the corporation, according to the framework. This translates into a specific problem for managers: find a way to overcome decisionmaking limitations. Unless these limitations are mitigated, the reasoning continues, the survival of the corporation is in jeopardy. Accordingly, the very reason for the Planning Process framework is the need to compensate for what McGowan, Liedtke, Ferris, MacPhail, and we cannot do individually: see the world by ourselves in sufficient detail to make intelligent strategic choices.[10] The Planning Process framework provides a way to find those details. We now turn to two basic variations on the process theme.[11]

TWO PLANNING PROCESS SOLUTIONS

Planning Process models come in a variety of flavors. Common across all these models is a concern for helping managers cope with the complexities of their companies' environments. We should not be surprised then that the different models reflect differing assumptions about how much leeway managers have in developing strategies and where that leeway is "granted" by the environment. Among the community of researchers who study Planning Process, two different interpretations have emerged regarding this leeway. As an introduction to these two perspectives, consider the following analogy between a senior executive and the conductor of a symphony orchestra.

For the conductor and the members of his orchestra, the centerpiece of their interrelationship is the musical score. The score provides a blueprint by which the conductor and musicians collaborate in the production of a satisfying musical performance. Satisfying performance, of course, is a measure of what not only the conductor and musicians, but also the audience and critics, want and expect to hear. The score is performed in the context of an environment—audience members, for example—that can affect the performers. Moving to the Planning Process framework, the conductor becomes the senior executive and the score becomes the specific planning process that the executive wants employees to adopt. The two Planning Process variations differ regarding what the executive/ conductor should do with the process/score.[12]

One approach is to view the score as a sequence of activities—movements, passages, and so on—undertaken by various members of the orchestra. The conductor's objective is to get through the score faithfully, efficiently, seamlessly. Positive feedback from the audience is welcomed, of course, but not essential to the orchestra's task. For all parties concerned, thus, beautiful music is the consequence of following the score.

A Formal Strategic Planning (hereafter, Formal) variation on the Planning Process framework bears a close resemblance to this conception of an orchestra's efforts. In the Formal scheme, the planning process is a linear progression of activities. Environmental complexity surely provides the grist for those process activities, but does not unduly restrict managers in moving from one step to the next. To the Formal planner, the company's environment is changing, but strategic plans can be put together under relatively controlled conditions.[13]

Making beautiful music can be understood in a radically different light, however. Flutists, violinists, oboists, and members of the audience have their good days and their bad days. The conductor knows that he can be "on" or "off," as well. When he raises his baton, he very well may not know what will happen next. His objective, from this perspective, is to get through the score successfully. The score is not so much a set of instructions, but a rough outline of how to proceed. It is, for the conductor, all that stands between him and complete chaos.[14]

An Evolutionary variation on the Planning Process framework captures this analogy to symphony music. In the Evolutionary scheme, planning processes cannot proceed linearly because the organization's environment is simply too unpredictable. Managers should have formal processes, therefore, for responding to unforeseeable events. In other words, "planning process" is synonymous with the Boy Scout motto: be prepared (for the unexpected).[15]

The Formal and Evolutionary variations both emphasize adherence to specific procedures for developing a strategy. It may well be that one approach can be useful in relatively stable contexts and the other can be helpful in more chaotic cases. We are not concerned here with that proposition, however. [16] Instead, we want you to understand what the Planning Process framework can contribute in the context of our principles about persons, business basics, and timely strategic action.

Formal Planning Process

Formal planning is a continual activity conducted at multiple levels of the organization in a "planning cycle."[17] The five-step logic behind this process is known to anyone who has ever read about conventional management practice:

1. Set objectives.
2. Generate alternative strategies for achieving objectives.
3. Analyze the pros and cons of each alternative.
4. Select the best strategic alternative.
5. Prepare appropriate plans, budgets, cash flow statements, and so on.

Planning Process models have proliferated around these themes. Some models simplify the scheme; others contain dozens of steps and hundreds of interconnections.[18] All such Formal models point to the linear development of some rough ideas into a full-fledged strategic plan.

One of the better known Formal models has been developed by Peter Lorange and Richard Vancil.[19] They specify the seven-step approach, which links corporate-level and SBU-level planning, that is shown in Figure 7–1.[20] A return to the Allegis case will help depict how the Formal planning logic works.

Formal Planning and Allegis. Suppose that Richard Ferris decides to adopt the Lorange–Vancil model after adding Hertz and Hilton to United Airlines. As we meet him in Step 1 (see Figure 7–1) of the planning cycle, Ferris is evaluating the strengths and weaknesses of Allegis as a whole. By matching his internal analysis with a corresponding assessment of Allegis's environment, he can produce what Lorange calls a "corporate gap analysis" for Allegis.[21] General strategic guidelines are then set to fill this gap. If this all sounds very much like the Harvard Policy framework, it is, because Lorange and Vancil do, in fact, seek to extend that logic.

This extension is readily apparent in Step 2 where Ferris applies the same internal and external scrutiny for Hertz, Hilton, and United as separate SBUs (see Chapter 4). Where gaps between SBU capability and market opportunity are identified, the SBU managers and their staffs devise appropriate, broadly based strategic programs. It is at this point, for example, that United executives might identify the need to enhance United's trans-Pacific or East Coast market presence.

Figure 7–1. A Basic Formal Strategic Planning Cycle.

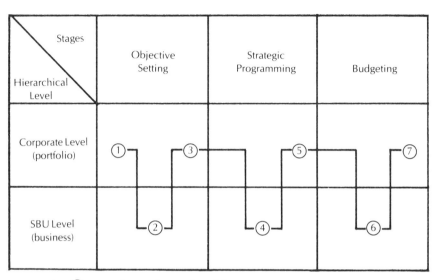

Stages / Hierarchical Level	Objective Setting	Strategic Programming	Budgeting
Corporate Level (portfolio)	① ③	⑤	⑦
SBU Level (business)	②	④	⑥

Major Tasks: ① Formulation of general guidelines
② Formulation of board strategic action programs
③ Consolidation of action programs
④ Generation, evaluation, and selection of strategic programs
⑤ Consolidation of strategic programs
⑥ Development of tactical programs and budgets
⑦ Consolidation of budgets

Source: Peter Lorange, *Implementation of Strategic Planning,* © 1982, p. 146. Reprinted by permission of Prentice-Hall, Inc., Englewood Cliffs, NJ.

Strategy deliberations at Allegis return to the corporate level where, in Step 3, Ferris and his staff consolidate the various SBU programs. Here, Ferris checks for the internal consistency—for Allegis as a whole—of the SBU plans. Once this has been accomplished, Ferris uses the model to oversee a process in which broad goals are translated into specific strategic programs (Steps 4 and 5) and corporate budgets (Steps 6 and 7). Throughout, the Lorange–Vancil model leads Ferris back and forth between corporate-level and SBU-level issues. This feature, coupled with the inclusion of budgeting deliberations, provides a more comprehensive approach to planning than is available from the Harvard Policy framework.

One of the major functions performed by a Formal system in a multibusiness organization is to provide a common language system that facilitates the interconnection of several strategies. In other words, Ferris can use a Formal model as a communications channel across all of Allegis. If put together with a company-wide perspective, a Formal model provides consistency in format, methods, and deadlines at multiple organizational levels. It is easily integrated with other administrative systems (e.g., accounting and budgeting, executive performance appraisal, management by objectives, etc.). Not only can a Formal model enable a Hertz SBU manager to converse with a counterpart at United, the model can involve lower-level managers directly in the process. In this way, the Lorange–Vancil approach differs from the more insulated planning discussions portrayed in the Harvard framework. In planning jargon, Formal models can promote "bottom up" planning in addition to, or in place of, the Harvard "top down" approach.

Evolutionary Planning Process

If Ferris were to seek advice instead from an advocate of the Evolutionary approach to Planning Process, he would hear a different story. Making strategy is a messy and uncertain process, he would be told, because, contrary to the Formal planner's belief, the world will not hold still long enough for Ferris to complete a planning cycle on his own terms. Sometimes the strategic directions that he initially intends will, in the end, be the route that Allegis may follow; sometimes this will not be the case.[22] Given the unpredictability in Allegis's environment, Ferris would learn, he is better off if he accepts the fact that strategies emerge, or evolve, from a complex interplay of forces. To the Evolutionary planner, then, flexibility is a virtue.

Although nothing in this Evolutionary approach denies the importance of planning process, the Evolutionary planner entertains a different concept of planning process. More to the point, he proposes a more complex planning process than does the Formal planner, a process replete with more steps, more feedback loops, and the like. One of the better known Evolutionary models is the "logical incrementalism" approach developed by James Brian Quinn.

As the label implies, Quinn's approach is a cautious one. Go slowly and delay making commitments until you must, he would advise Ferris.[23] In an elaborate, fourteen-activity model, Quinn describes strategic plan-

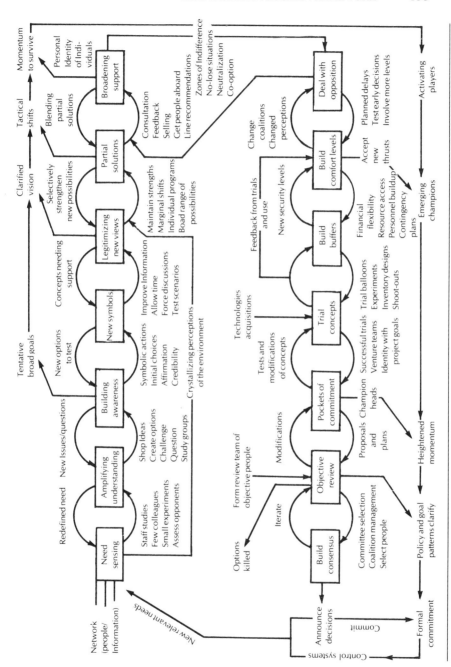

Source: James Brian Quinn, *Strategies for Change: Logical Incrementalism* (Homewood, Ill.: Richard D. Irwin), p. 104. Copyright © Richard D. Irwin, Inc., 1980. Reprinted with permission.

ning as a concurrent and never-ending mix of goal formation and program development.[24] The logical incrementalism model is depicted in Figure 7–2, where an "inner" pattern of activities—from need-sensing activities through consensus building—gradually produces an "outer" progression from tentative goals to formal organizational commitment to a strategy. Once again, logical incrementalism is clearly a process solution to strategy, differing from the Formal approach only in terms of relative complexity. That complexity is designed to enable Ferris to take strategic action in a complicated world.

A CRITICAL ANALYSIS OF THE PLANNING PROCESS FRAMEWORK

We suggested at the outset of this chapter that the Planning Process framework—with its emphasis on technique—might address timely managerial action in a way that other strategy frameworks cannot. Thus, our critical analysis will examine how well the framework deals with the Principle of Timely Action. Before we get to that point, however, there are two preliminary matters to consider: the object of the Planning Process framer's attention; and the resulting implications for our Principle about Persons and Principle of Business Basics.

Strategy in the Planning Process Framework

The Planning Process framework treats strategy quite differently than do any of the frameworks presented in Chapters 3 through 6. In the Harvard Policy framework, a strategy is a pattern of specific decisions. In the two economic frameworks, a strategy is a relationship between the company and the industry environment. In the Stakeholder Management framework, a strategy is a plan for action held in place by mutual agreements among stakeholders.[25]

Strategy is only incidental to the Planning Process framework, on the other hand.[26] The framework deals with the *act* of decisionmaking, but not a decision per se. This is a crucial distinction. Moreover, since a strategy is only one kind of decision, the framework is actually a generic approach that sheds little light on strategy per se.

Instead, the Planning Process framework is centrally concerned with the development and maintenance of the *planning process,* or *system,* at a company. According to the framework, the executive's musical score is the planning process, not the strategy produced by the process. The manager's job is to get the process right. This focus has significant implications in the context of our Principle about Persons and Principle of Business Basics and, eventually, the Principle of Timely Action.

A Principle About Persons

We meet very few persons in the Planning Process story. True, planning processes are designed to be orchestrated by persons like McGowan, Liedtke, Ferris, and MacPhail. Yet, their roles are merely to keep the planning system moving along at some vigorous—the Formal variation—or cautious—the Evolutionary variation—pace. Unlike the Harvard Policy framework where a place is reserved for top managers' values, there is no room in Figures 7–1 and 7–2 for the aims that McGowan et al. have for themselves and their constituents. Managers are merely stewards of a process here.[27]

None of this should be particularly surprising news. The framework is based on the assumptions that McGowan, Liedtke, Ferris, MacPhail, and everyone else need assistance in overcoming their innate bounded rationality and satisficing limitations. True, the framework implies that some managers can rise above the crowd and, with a special style or flair, derive better strategies from their planning processes than others can.[28] The implication, though, is that managers can make a difference only at the *margin* of planning processes, not in any central way. In short, the framework provides only passing attention to our Principle about Persons.

A Principle of Business Basics

There is a peculiar parochialism to the Planning Process framework as well. All the planning activities, whether of the Formal or Evolutionary variety, occur *within the walls of a single company*.[29] All the steps shown in Figures 7–1 and 7–2 are shots that a company's senior executives are presumably free to call. The musical score, in other words, is a private affair between the conductor and the orchestra. This suggests a great deal about the role of business basics in the Planning Process framework.

Product quality, customer service, and competition are incidental to the Planning Process framework. It is certainly true that planning systems are designed to provide a systematic means for understanding such environmental factors. However, the framework provides no specific insights on the business basics. Each factor is alike, valued simply as a source of information to be processed.

In this context, the Planning Process advocate is content to think about the company's environment in broad, aggregate terms. We have already seen the consequences of this with the Harvard Policy framework. Both frameworks imply that it is sufficient for McGowan to keep abreast of broad trends in telecommunications competition, but not deButts' specific alternatives. Both frameworks imply that Ferris should concentrate on trends in business travel, but not what drives travel agents in Florida and business persons going through O'Hare Airport in Chicago. Furthermore, the Planning Process framework—regardless of the variety—does not provide for recurring interaction with the persons whose concrete actions make up the business basics. Once action programs have been consolidated in the Lorange–Vancil model (see Figure 7–1), managers are guided by the framework to leave the business environment behind. Once the matter of "crystallizing perceptions of the environment" is accomplished in the logical incrementalism model (see Figure 7–2, center), managers are guided away from the business environment and business basics, as well. The framework instead quickly diverts a manager's attention in another direction. This diversion and the reason for it take us to the heart of the timely action issue.

A Principle of Timely Action

Gaining employee commitment is a primary goal of the Planning Process framework. After broadly surveying environmental trends, Ferris should, according to the framework, refocus his efforts on employee commitment. But, we encounter a subtle twist here. In the Harvard Policy and Stakeholder Management frameworks, employees commit themselves, or do not commit themselves, to a strategy. Since the Planning Process framework deals with the strategy process, but not a strategy, employee commitment must mean something different.[30] In fact, it is employee commitment to the planning process that becomes the manager's primary worry, according to the framework. Put somewhat differently, the framework diverts a manager's attention from the business basics toward *implementing the process.*[31] *Yet, implementing the process and implementing a strategy can be two different things.* This diversion raises serious questions about whether the Planning Process framework can promote timely action. In fact, there are two logical reasons why it cannot do so.

First, timely strategic action is not possible if the key players have not found reason to cooperate. Unlike the Stakeholder Management framework, the Planning Process framework is confined to what happens inside a company. It is unlikely then that a manager who uses this framework will identify, much less be able to persuade, others who have reason to resist the strategy.

In this way, the framework provides a false sense of timely action. Ferris can be quite effective in getting his executives to "sign up" for the planning process that, when implemented, produces the Allegis plan. However, that process excludes the Coniston Partners, Donald Trump, and perhaps the United pilots. The framework cannot help Ferris take timely action in this larger context which, in the end, proved crucial. The second logical problem with the framework contains the reason for this.

Timely action implies that a manager has room to maneuver with alternatives; it also implies that managers can act when they judge action to be necessary, and that managers have some intended future outcome in mind when they choose to act. The Planning Process framework, whatever the variety, is aimed at squelching all three elements of timely action. *Control over managerial action, rather than liberation of managerial action, is the dominant theme in the Planning Process framework.* This is the reason why implementing the process is so vital in the framework. It is also the reason why timely action runs against the grain of planning process.

Logical incrementalism is a vivid illustration of this. The whole point of Quinn's argument is that managers should *not* commit to a course of action too hastily. What could be more discouraging to timely action than a fourteen-step procedure (see Figure 7–2) that curtails a manager's room to maneuver, provides no room for a manager's judgment, and does not deal with strategy per se! In this way, logical incrementalism reflects a problem present in all variations of the Planning Process logic: controlling the variability in managers' actions takes on such overriding importance that attention is diverted from persons and the business basics. It should come as no surprise then that timely action plays a lesser role, as well.

CONCLUSION

The Planning Process framework provides a systematic logic for assembling the relevant data that managers need in their strategic deliberations. This emphasis is appealing, insofar as the Harvard Policy, Portfolio, Competitive Strategy, and Stakeholder Management frameworks devote less attention to the techniques of strategy-making. We hypothesized that the framework might shed light on timely action where the other frameworks could not.

However, our hopes were overly optimistic. A stiff price must be paid by managers who choose to take advantage of the detail offered in the Planning Process framework. That price includes specific attention to persons and the business basics, as well as, due to the central importance of process control in the framework, a blueprint for timely action. Before we abandon the idea that *how* managers plan makes a difference, we now turn to a recently developed framework that places planning in a larger context.

NOTES TO CHAPTER 7

1. James Brian Quinn's assertion sets the tone here: "Since there is no objectively right answer concerning the proper ultimate ends for an organization, sensible practice dictates giving top priority to the *processes* through which such choices are made." The emphasis is Quinn's. See James Brian Quinn, *Strategies for Change: Logical Incrementalism* (Homewood, Ill.: Richard D. Irwin, 1980), p. 181. For an analysis that exposes the non sequitur in arguments made by Quinn and many social scientists, see Alasdair MacIntyre, *After Virtue*, 2d ed. (Notre Dame, Ind.: University of Notre Dame Press, 1984), pp. 23–35. In MacIntyre's terms, Quinn gives a classic emotivist account.

2. The subtlety here is that this conception of strategy is not centrally concerned *with* strategy, but rather with processes for making strategy. Discussions with Professor Andrew Van de Ven have been influential here.

3. We are indebted to our colleague, S. Venkataraman, for his assistance with this chapter.

4. This is to say that the effectiveness of planning processes might be measured in terms of a manager's ability to "connect the dots." We find it very interesting that some Planning Process researchers, most notably Peter Lorange, are uneasy with this measure. See Peter Lorange, *Corporate Planning: An Executive Viewpoint* (Englewood Cliffs, N.J.: Prentice-Hall, 1980), pp. 280–82.

5. For a classic rendition of such research, see Andrew H. Van de Ven, "Problem Solving, Planning, and Innovation. Part I. Test of the Program Planning Model," *Human Relations* 33, no. 10 (1980): 711–40.

6. What follows provides vivid testimony to the absence of a critical tradition in strategy research. The two assumptions in question have been adopted, without much debate, from Herbert Simon's writings forty years ago. A discussion with Professor Lance Kurke has helped us understand this point.

7. See Herbert A. Simon, *Administrative Behavior*, Third Edition (New York: Free Press, 1976), pp. xxviii–xxxi, pp. 38–41.

8. Ibid.

9. Our point is simply that researchers can choose to consider persons as either (1) generally capable of self-motivated achievement or (2) generally in need of some external kick. Bounded rationality and satisficing frame the discussion *either way*. Researchers can either celebrate human potential, or seek to curtail it. The dominant contemporary choice, Peters and Waterman notwithstanding, has been the latter, Orwellian theme.

10. Many strategy researchers are indebted to Herbert Simon for the premise that rational choice must be equivalent to omniscience. Thus, the cards are stacked against the decisionmaker from the start, in this research genre.

11. This interpretation draws upon Henry Mintzberg and James A. Waters, "Of Strategies, Deliberate and Emergent," *Strategic Management Journal* 6, no. 3 (1985): 257–72.

12. For insights into this approach to the problem, see Stanley Fish, *Is There a Text in This Class?*, (Cambridge, Mass.: Harvard University Press, 1980).

13. One illustration of this is given in W. Brooke Tunstall, *Disconnecting Parties: Managing the Bell System Break-up: An Inside View* (New York: McGraw-Hill, 1985). Tunstall's title is apt. He assumes that the story of divestiture implementation can be told as solely an internal decisionmaking problem at AT&T.

14. Discussions with Professor Sharlyn Orbaugh about a Japanese concept of chaos have helped shape this point for us.

15. Research in this genre is often focused on finding the elusive structural determinants of some aboriginal force known as "change."

16. Put somewhat differently, the usefulness of *change* as a reference point for research also needs to be justified in critical debate. Our three principles suggest, however, that change is a second-order condition that results from persons interacting with other persons to make up relationships that we call "business basics."

17. The principal reference here is Peter Lorange, *Implementation of Strategic Planning* (Englewood Cliffs, N.J.: Prentice-Hall, 1979). Many, many versions of this cycle idea have been published. If your company has fifteen-month planning calendars and the like, you undoubtedly know about the cycle metaphor already.

18. See, for example, Robert A. Burgelman, "A Process Model of Internal Corporate Venturing in the Diversified Major Firm," *Administrative Science Quarterly* 28, no. 2 (1983): 223–44.

19. See Peter Lorange and Richard F. Vancil, "How to Design a Strategic Planning System," *Harvard Business Review* 54, no. 5 (1976): 75–81.

20. This can, of course, be extended to more and more detailed subdivisions of the firm. See, for example, Lorange, *Corporate Planning: An Executive Viewpoint*, pp. 54–60.

21. See Lorange, *The Implementation of Strategic Planning*, p. 146.

22. This is the reminder that runs throughout the argument in Mintzberg and Waters, "Of Strategies, Deliberate and Emergent."

23. Certainly, Quinn couches his "advice" in terms of descriptive research; that is, what managers "really do," as opposed to what "normative research" indicates that they should do. This is a false distinction, however, if we view research models as possible interpretations of a manager's world. By *choosing* to tell his story this way, Quinn has entered the world of normative research. For an enlightening introduction to this point, see Richard Rorty, *Consequences of Pragmatism* (Minneapolis, Minn.: University of Minnesota Press, 1982), pp. 90–99.

24. See Quinn, *Strategies for Change: Logical Incrementalism*, p. 104.

25. See Daniel R. Gilbert, Jr., and Carol K. Jacobson, "Stakeholders, Ideology, and Enterprise Strategy" (Paper for Annual Meeting, Academy of Management, New Orleans, Louisiana, August, 1987).

26. See Daniel R. Gilbert, Jr., "Strategy and Justice" (Ph.D. diss., University of Minnesota), chap. 5.

27. In fact, managers are generally characterized as sources of error, even nuisances, in this genre. Read through Lorange, *Corporate Planning: An Executive Viewpoint*, and see how managerial characters are portrayed.

28. But, this is only to acknowledge that managers are external sources of variation, and not central players in the Planning Process story.

29. For a discussion of this curious isolationism, see Daniel R. Gilbert, Jr., "The Mystery of the AT&T Divestiture," in R. Grover, ed. *Proceedings* (Midwest Academy of Management, 1987), pp. 26–30.

30. This is another way of saying that the Planning Process framework pays lip service, at best, to Chester Barnard's conception of employee commitment as the product of bargaining.

31. See Gilbert, "Strategy and Justice," chap. 6. The distinction here is quite evident in the Harvard Policy arguments about strategy.

ANNOTATED BIBLIOGRAPHY

The Planning Process framework includes many variations on the basic theme of orderly decisionmaking in an uncertain world. The following collection provides a comprehensive introduction.

Allison, Graham T. *Essence of Decision*. Boston, Mass.: Little, Brown, 1971.

Miles, Raymond E., and Charles Snow. *Organizational Strategy, Structure, and Process*. New York: McGraw-Hill, 1978.

Miles, Robert H. *Coffin Nails and Corporate Strategy*. Englewood Cliffs, N.J.: Prentice-Hall, 1982.

Quinn, James Brian; Henry Mintzberg; and Robert M. James. *The Strategy Process*. Englewood Cliffs, N.J.: Prentice-Hall, 1988.

Schendel, Dan E., and Charles W. Hofer, eds. *Strategic Management: A New View of Business Policy and Planning*. Boston, Mass.: Little, Brown, 1979.

8 THE SEVEN-S FRAMEWORK

Allegis stands as stark testimony that creative attempts at corporate strategy can be for naught. In fact, the business landscape is littered with strategies that, while eminently sensible and coherent in some sense, simply could not be translated into lasting, organized programs. Moreover, the fact that many ill-fated strategies are produced from structured decisionmaking processes (see Chapter 7) seems to cast doubt on the worth of planning processes.

On the basis of this evidence, Robert Waterman, Thomas Peters, Julien Phillips, and Anthony Athos, among others, have proposed that managers must understand strategy in a context that includes far more than simply the procedures for making strategy.[1] Waterman et al. propose the Seven-S framework as one way to rescue planning process.[2]

In one respect, the Seven-S framework represents a direct challenge to the basic proposition in the Planning Process framework that adhering to a coherent decisionmaking process will produce an effective strategy. Waterman et al. argue that this proposition is too simplistic. Strategy and decisionmaking processes (or structure), they claim, are but two of seven organizational factors that can influence a company's success or lack of it.[3] That is, strategy and structure, when joined with *s*ystems, *s*tyle, *s*kills, *s*taff, and *s*uperordinate goals, make up a pattern that managers must somehow balance.[4] This seven-part alliteration gives rise to the "Seven-S" label.

In another respect, however, the Seven-S framework shares a common conceptual basis with the Planning Process framework. Both approaches stress the severe limitations imposed on managers by the human tendencies toward bounded rationality and satisficing behavior (see Chapter 7).[5] Thus, both frameworks are built on the premise that managers need considerable structured guidance to make important decisions about their companics' futures.[6] While the Seven-S framers argue that planning process is more circular than the Formal and Evolutionary approaches (see Chapter 7) suggest, do not be misled on the key point here. Seven-S, like the Planning Process framework, provides a story about structured decisionmaking.

THE BASIC IDEA

Each "S" factor in the Seven-S framework represents a particular feature of a company. *Structure* deals with how work tasks are divided and then coordinated. *Strategy* involves selecting some combination of products for some set of markets. *Systems* are those organizational procedures that managers use to control structure and strategy. *Style* refers to the way that managers spend their time and to their use of symbolic action. How employees are socialized into adopting and following a company's style is a matter of *staff*. The capability of employees to do all this is a *skills* issue. Finally, senior executives choose some *superordinate goals* on which the company is united. Waterman et al. suggest that the framework is sufficiently flexible to allow one to "enter the company" through any one factor and wind his way to the other six. Our interest here, of course, is with the strategy "S." Consider how we might look at Pennzoil and the Minnesota Twins organizations from this perspective.

Hugh Liedtke decided to stand toe-to-toe with McKinley and McKinley's successors at Texaco. We might identify Liedtke's strategy in these terms: wait until Pennzoil is paid fair compensation for the loss of Getty.[7] Andy MacPhail decided to take a less strident stance regarding the Minnesota Twins' competitors. Rather than add a twenty-fifth player and risk retaliation by his counterparts at other teams, he decided on this strategy: solve the team's pitching problems within the twenty-four player limit, while conducting frequent auditions for the occupant of the twenty-fourth spot.

For Liedtke and MacPhail, the Seven-S framework provides both a cautionary guideline and a basic proposition. According to Seven-S, any strategy is conditioned by the six other "Ss."[8] If Liedtke and MacPhail overlook the influence of organizational systems and their companies' skills, for example, they run the risk of proceeding with an ill-advised strategy. The multiple influences on any one "S" factor are shown in Figure 8–1 where each "S" is ultimately connected with every other "S."

Figure 8–1.   The Seven-S Framework.

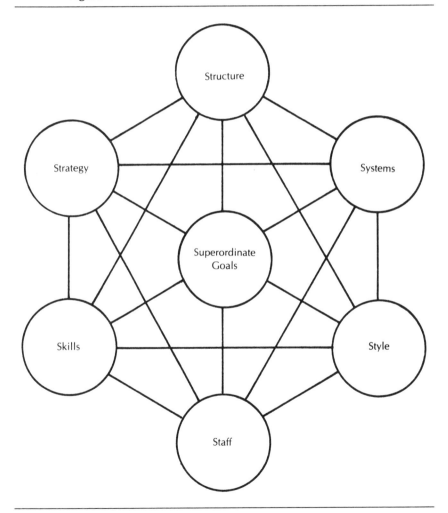

Source: Robert H. Waterman, Jr., Thomas J. Peters, and Julien R. Phillips, "Structure Is Not Organization," *Business Horizons* 23, no. 3 (June 1980): 18. Reprinted with permission.

A Basic Proposition

A basic Seven-S proposition holds that strategic success will vary with the alignment of, or fit among, the seven "S" factors.[9] If MacPhail's strategy is consistent with the Twins' structure, systems, style, skills, staff, and subordinate goals, then his plan of action should be a winner. According to the framework, *how* a strategy is developed remains important, but developing a strategy is a more complicated problem than the Planning Process framework suggests. This complexity will become obvious as we narrate the Seven-S version of Liedtke's and MacPhail's stories.

SEVEN FACTORS IN A ROW

Waterman et al. suggest that the Seven-S framework starts with some underlying theme that guides all the company's activities.[10] Such a *superordinate goal* provides a rallying point for each of the other six factors. Starting here, and focusing on strategy, let's see how Liedtke and MacPhail should act if they want to be Seven-S managers.

Seven-S at Pennzoil

Suppose that Liedtke and his senior officers all endorse, in word and deed, an overarching goal of rapid growth in Pennzoil's size. That particular superordinate goal and Liedtke's "wait" strategy seem to be aligned if the probability of collecting from Texaco is high. If so, the fit between strategy and superordinate goal is plausible.

Next, Liedtke must ensure that Pennzoil's organizational structure is consistent with his decision to wait for payment. He could accomplish this by setting up a special task force charged with the day-to-day management of the stalemate with Texaco.[11] In this way, the ongoing petroleum operations at Pennzoil are not impeded. Closely related to the strategy-structure alignment is the matter of organizational systems at Pennzoil. If Liedtke wants to send a clear signal to McKinley, Kinnear, and DeCrane that he is prepared to wait, then he surely wants to control public pronouncements from his managers. If a Pennzoil officer were to hint, much less come out and announce, that Pennzoil's position is negotiable, Liedtke's strategy would shatter. In Seven-S terms, Liedtke needs to arrange Pennzoil's public relations system so that the strategy is not undermined. Other systems must be aligned with the strategy as well. Managers in the special "stalemate" task force will probably be compensated differently than standard for marketing managers.

Once Liedtke is confident that Pennzoil's superordinate goal, structure, and systems are all consistent with the strategy, he moves on to match Pennzoil's style, staff, and skills with the strategy. All this is actually oversimplified. According to the framework, Liedtke must also make sure that, given the "wait" strategy, the appropriate systems and staff responses, for example, are consistent as well. The problems in aligning style, staff, and skills are vividly illustrated in MacPhail's case.

Seven-S and Woeful Pitching

Suppose that MacPhail is confident that his strategy is supported by a superordinate goal and appropriate structure and systems. When he turns to the issue of style, he must consider the behavioral tendencies of the field manager, the baseball equivalent of a chief operating officer. When MacPhail considers staff issues, the Seven-S framework points to the way Twins players are typically socialized into becoming team members. MacPhail must assess whether the Twins' potent offensive skills can carry the team through its pitching difficulties. If the matches among style, staff, and skills are poor, according to Seven-S, then the effect on the Twins' strategy can be disastrous. Consider one hypothetical example of this.

MacPhail's strategy puts a premium on the patience (style) of his manager and players. Woeful pitching usually translates into losing streaks. Impatient players can become demoralized over losing and pay less attention to the offensive competency (skills) of the team, thereby further contributing to the losing streak.

Major league baseball players typically serve apprenticeships in a team's organization before reaching the major league level. During that period, team executives often seek to socialize these players into doing things "our way." Many of the 1986 Twins players had, in fact, been together throughout their careers. Now, MacPhail's search for pitching help will probably lead him to hire pitchers who were socialized elsewhere. According to Seven-S, MacPhail can run into major problems if he does not align his players' socialization lessons (staff) with their patience (style) during the low points in the 1986 season. Among other things, MacPhail may need to explain his moves carefully to the longer term members of the Twins "family." If he neglects to do so, his entire strategy could unravel.

A CRITICAL ANALYSIS OF THE
SEVEN-S FRAMEWORK

By now, it should be clear that the Seven-S framework provides a comprehensive context. The basic message from Seven-S is that all seven factors must flow in the same direction. But, what does it mean to arrange these factors "in the same direction"? It is one thing to propose a framework—as Waterman et al. do—with no clear linear progression from factor to factor. It is quite another matter, however, to ignore the need for some standards(s) against which "direction" can be judged effective or not. Is the Seven-S framework logically complete?

The framework suggests two avenues of meaning for "in the same direction." One points to superordinate goals and suggests viewing such goals as base points against which the other six S factors can be aligned. Waterman et al. resist such a move to single out one "super S" from among six "dwarf Ss."[12] As a consequence, they apparently rule out superordinate goals as sources of standards, or decision rules, in getting the seven Ss correct.[13]

This leaves open a second possibility. Like the Stakeholder Management framework, the Seven-S model could appeal to some standard external to the framework. In the Stakeholder case (see Chapter 6), we noted that the door was opened to applying an ethical analysis to persons and business basics. In search of some external standards for Seven-S, let's turn to what the framework has to say about our three principles.

Seven-S and Our Logic for Strategy

Our assessment here will be brief, because the Seven-S framework deals tangentially, at best, with our Principle about Persons and Principle of Business Basics. Moreover, the framework invites the same potential for analysis paralysis—and, hence, violation of our Principle of Timely Action—that is present in other frameworks.

First, the seven factors are clearly organizational attributes, not individual ones. The Seven-S analysis is conducted at such a broad level of aggregation that individual motivations and actions are buried. True, Liedtke and MacPhail can use the framework, but they are not visible *in* the framework in any sophisticated sense.

Second, the Seven-S framework applies solely within a single company. Like its Planning Process cousin, Seven-S considers the business basics—customers, competitors, and employees—to be *secondary sources* of data for managers. As with Planning Process, the Seven-S framework implies that managers can deal with the business basics from the comfortable confines of the executive suite. There is no counterpart to stakeholder transactions in either the Planning Process or Seven-S frameworks.

Finally, timely action seems secondary in the Seven-S framework. The interconnectedness of the seven Ss is clear evidence of this. If our rusty statistical skills are still to be trusted, we calculate that seven Ss translate into twenty-one possible relationships among any two S factors. The potential for paralyzing analytical cycles is impressive, especially when we add this maze of interconnections to the framework's silence about standards for aligning the seven Ss.

CONCLUSION

The Seven-S framework is intended to challenge the proposition that efficient planning processes produce effective strategies. A comprehensive context for strategic action and a flexible formula for decisionmaking are two advantages that await those managers who apply the Seven-S ideas. Yet, the flexibility comes at a severe cost. Nothing in the framework provides specific guidance about the meaning of aligning all seven factors. Moreover, none of the three principles in our logic for strategy—three possible standards by which Ss could be made consistent—is very important in the Seven-S scheme. The framework simply trades off flexibility for any meaningful insights about persons, business basics, and timely action in the context of strategy.

NOTES TO CHAPTER 8

1. See, for example, Thomas J. Peters and Robert H. Waterman, Jr., *In Search of Excellence* (New York: Harper & Row, 1982), and Richard T. Pascale and Anthony G. Athos, *The Art of Japanese Management: Applications for American Executives* (New York: Simon and Schuster, 1981).

2. The principal source is Robert H. Waterman, Jr., Thomas J. Peters, and Julien R. Phillips, "Structure Is Not Organization," *Business Horizons*, June 1980, pp. 14–26.
3. Note that all this analysis applies to the organization, not persons.
4. See Waterman, Peters, and Phillips, "Structure Is Not Organization." If you are looking for an interpretation of "balance," the authors do not help you.
5. The "severe limitations" imagery comes from Herbert A. Simon, *Administrative Behavior*, 3d ed. (New York: Free Press, 1976), p. 102.
6. Ibid. Simon refers to this as the need to institutionalize persons.
7. See, for example, Thomas Petzinger, Jr., "Pennzoil Board Cool to Texaco's Settlement Offer," *Wall Street Journal*, April 25, 1986, p. 4.
8. See Waterman, Peters, and Phillips, "Structure Is Not Organization," pp. 17–18. Again, it is factors, not persons, that interact here.
9. No concept of "fit" is provided in the framework, however.
10. See Waterman, Peters, and Phillips, "Structure Is Not Organization," pp. 24–25. This claim seems to contradict their assertion that there is no logical beginning or ending in the Seven-S circle.
11. Ibid., pp. 19–20.
12. There is no justification given by the authors for this position.
13. Once again, the flight from standards rears its head in strategy research. See R. Edward Freeman and the Daniel R. Gilbert, Jr., *Corporate Strategy and the Search for Ethics* (Englewood Cliffs, N.J.: Prentice-Hall, 1988), chap. 2.

ANNOTATED BIBLIOGRAPHY

Peters and Waterman have each recently published extensions of their basic arguments in the spirit of Seven-S. Both have made it onto the *New York Times Book Review* Best-Sellers list.

Peters, Tom. *Thriving on Chaos*. New York: Alfred A. Knopf, 1987.
Waterman, Robert H., Jr. *The Renewal Factor*. New York: Bantam, 1987.

9 A SEARCH FOR A LOGIC FOR STRATEGY

Many persons have written many words about strategy. We can all gain a valuable insight into these writings if we take a few minutes to recall the well-known story about Humpty Dumpty. Humpty's frame, you'll remember, was damaged beyond repair in his fall from the wall. None of the characters in the story could reassemble Humpty as they knew him, and we are left to draw our own conclusions about the unfortunate, fragmented egg.

Now, writing about strategy certainly involves taking apart some aspect of the concept and examining the pieces from different angles. Yet, many, many persons who write about strategy seem intent upon revising the ending to the Humpty Dumpty tale. They value tidy stories. They find discomfort in the possibility that pieces of eggshell might remain scattered on the ground. So, in a grand flourish predicated upon some new insight or a key piece of missing data, they dutifully try to put the old egg back together in a new and improved way.

All this is to say that integration, or synthesis, is the paramount goal among many who write about strategy. Indeed, the compelling urge to integrate concepts, frameworks, whatever, has become the hallmark of progress in management research. Grand theories and grand collections of data are the holy grails. Synthesis is very much in fashion.[1]

ASKING A DIFFERENT QUESTION

There is a basic problem with this widespread approach. We cannot develop sophisticated understandings about strategy—or any management concept—if we view synthesis in isolation. Synthesis *is* important, if we want to see our world in some coherent way. However, we must all be willing to consider the possibility, as disconcerting as it might be, that some ideas are like the scattered pieces of Humpty Dumpty: they *cannot* be combined in any meaningful way.

Admitting to this possibility is hard, but it is all the more difficult, and crucial, to search for the places where the pieces do not fit. We must be willing to ask a different kind of question in this context. Instead of looking at two concepts and only asking "What is similar here?", we must also be prepared to ask *"What is different here?"* [2] Only then can we intelligently take the necessary steps to combine concepts into coherent stories about the world in which we live.

The Purpose of This Chapter

In writing this book, we have been concerned with differences, rather than similarities, across six contemporary approaches to strategy. Throughout, our three principles have provided a vehicle for drawing distinctions. Consequently, the ending to this book will differ considerably from those of most other strategy books.

Do not look for a tidy synthesis of frameworks—a reconstructed egg, in other words—in the remaining pages. It isn't there. *This chapter explains that there are three very good reasons for not integrating the six frameworks.* Our purpose here is to review our findings about the state of the art in strategy. In the process, we will argue that the worth of a strategy framework need not depend on whether it complements another framework. We can offer a better standard with which to find a logic for strategy. [3]

THE STATE OF THE CONCEPT OF STRATEGY

We began the analysis in Chapter 1 by observing that more than a few people see little value in the concept of strategy. As we noted, the profusion of strategy models, one might argue, indicates that something is wrong with the basic concept. We have attempted to dispel this notion. Our first conclusion about the state of the art in strategy is this: *there is nothing inherently wrong with the concept of strategy*. It simply does not follow that a multitude of models (fact) implies a problem with the underlying concept (conclusion).[4]

Think back to Chapters 3 through 8. We have shown that six different interpretations of strategy can be derived from a basic notion well-known to the Greeks: advantages can await those who enter the future on some predetermined course. More specifically, we have shown how managers such as William McGowan can use any one of the six interpretations to make sense of his problems. Those six stories differ, of course. Any concept rich enough to spawn at least six diverse and usable perspectives on a manager's problems seems to be healthy.[5] If there are problems with any one story, it makes more sense to examine that story than to cast doubt upon strategy *per se*. We will return to this point shortly.

There is an important corollary here. Different conceptions of strategy can help managers sort problems into different contexts. In this way, they can sift through different ways to understand the issues and choose a course of intelligent action. Because the frameworks differ in some important respects, managers are better off if those stories remain distinct. In short, *there is no need to integrate some, or all, of the strategy frameworks*. The value of multiple, distinct perspectives is lost if managers and researchers succumb to the urge to tie everything together in some grand package.[6]

At the same time, we need to put this diversity into perspective. Without a way to evaluate the worth of any one strategy framework, managers cannot choose intelligently. More does not necessarily mean better when it comes to nuclear arsenals, government, and strategy frameworks.[7]

A CRITIQUE OF THE STRATEGY FRAMEWORKS

We argued in Chapter 1 that strategy is a familiar idea, even if the term has only recently been added to the language of business. We built this case by showing that a wide range of contexts for understanding strategy—prehistoric hunting grounds to Greek battlefields to corporate boardrooms to our own lives—could be united through three themes: the principles that deal with persons, business basics, and timely action.[8]

These principles are valuable in two respects. They not only provide a certain coherence to strategy, but they also prompt a question that few authors explicitly consider: Is this strategy framework worth applying?[9] As we analyzed the six frameworks, a second conclusion clearly emerged: *most of the six strategy frameworks fall short of satisfying the three principles in our logic for strategy.*

Two particular shortcomings stand out. First, only the Stakeholder Management and, to a lesser extent, the Harvard Policy frameworks deal with the Principle about Persons in any thorough and ongoing manner. In each of the other frameworks, human beings—including those who presumably can apply the frameworks in question—are missing from the action. Second, only the Competitive Strategy and Stakeholder Management frameworks provide comprehensive insights into such business basics as product quality, customer service, competition, and employee commitment. True, these business basics can be found in the Harvard Policy, Portfolio Strategy, Planning Process, and Seven-S approaches. But, in order to do so, all these factors must be integrated into aggregate measures of the company's environment. That can easily lead you overlooking such external factors as: (1) the alternatives being considered by a valuable customer; (2) the closest competitor's new ventures; and (3) employee reaction to the latest annual plan published in their newsletter. In short, there may be hidden costs in viewing the world through the lens of aggregate measures.

Strategy and the Single Company

A peculiar theme links these two broad criticisms of the six frameworks. With the exception of the Stakeholder Management framework, the frameworks all depict strategy as something that managers can accomplish *within a single company* and *on more or less their own timetable.* These frameworks give the impression that outsiders such as competitors, legislators, consumer advocates, and investigative reporters can be appeased, controlled, or even ignored while managers "do strategy." A familiar theme reappears here. Once again, the virtue of tidiness takes precedence as persons and business basics take a back seat.

Timely action takes a back seat as well. If strategy is something that managers can simply impose on their environments after a thorough decisionmaking process is conducted, timely action then becomes merely an internal checkpoint in that process. It is little wonder that the Principle of Timely Action fares poorly across the frameworks examined in Chapters 3 through 8.

Based on our analysis using the three principles, one corollary clearly follows: *some frameworks simply cannot be combined at certain junctures*. It would not be sensible to tie together, for example, the Competitive Strategy framework, which provides a reasonably comprehensive picture, and the Planning Process framework, in which the business basics fade into a set of parameters.

On a more hopeful note, our three principles indicate some advantages to developing two complementary frameworks. For those interested in gaining as broad an outlook as possible about business basics, the Competitive Strategy and Stakeholder Management frameworks share some common assumptions. If the Principle about Persons predominates, look to possible overlaps between the Harvard Policy and Stakeholder Management frameworks.[10] However, before patching any two ideas together, be willing to look for differences as well as similarities.

STRATEGY FRAMEWORKS AND MANAGERIAL JUDGMENT

Sooner or later, managers must put away the strategy framework, the calculator, and the strategic planning documents and decide on a course of action in the context of others doing the very same thing. The purpose of any framework, or interpretation, is to set up the problem.[11] We have shown six ways to do this. Certainly, there are many others. Yet, no framework can serve as a substitute for judgment. To do this, managers need something more than strategy framework—they need a logic for their own strategic actions.

We have provided one possible logic for strategy. We have argued that, no matter what else may be considered, it makes sense to base decisions on concerns for persons, business basics, and timely action. We have also shown that some of the better known strategy frameworks do not accommodate these particular themes very well. This suggests that a search for a logic for strategy is a search for two things.

First, think about the principles that can, or should, drive strategic activities. We believe that the Principle about Persons, the Principle of Business Basics, and the Principle of Timely Action constitute a useful point of departure.[12] Second, search for strategy frameworks that deal with the world in terms of those principles. If, for example, a manager wants to account for himself and other persons (that is, follow the Principle about Persons) certain frameworks that we have examined will simply stymie the efforts.

Because strategic action is based on persons' choices, the worth of a strategy framework must be measured in terms of how well that framework can help McGowan, Liedtke, Ferris, MacPhail, and us cope with the choices we all face.[13] Furthermore, how we choose to cope depends on the principles we choose to guide our actions. This provides a third and final reason for resisting the "integration mania" that grips management writing these days: *some strategy frameworks should not be integrated because they violate the principles that we choose to follow in coping with our worlds.*

NOTES TO CHAPTER 9

1. For an example of theoretical synthesis, see David Ulrich and Jay B. Barney, "Perspectives in Organizations: Resource Dependence, Efficiency, and Population," *Academy of Management Review* 9, no. 3 (1984): 471–81.
    A call for grand data bases is provided in John Freeman, "Data Quality and the Development of Organizational Social Science: An Editorial Essay," *Administrative Science Quarterly* 31, no. 1 (1986): 298–303.
2. For a readable discussion of this emergent emphasis in Western intellectual thought, see Mark Taylor, "Descartes, Nietzsche and the Search for the Unsayable," *New York Times Book Review*, February 1, 1987, pp. 3, 34.
3. By "better," we simply refer to attempts to understand the contexts in which one individually must choose and act.
4. Think of the concept of strategy as a seed from which offspring arise.
5. The key is usability, once again. Thus, the number of models is barely a necessary condition.
6. A classic, and disappointing, example of this can be found in the closing chapter of Graham T. Allison, *Essence of Decision* (Boston, Mass.: Little, Brown, 1971), where Allison succumbs to a synthetic urge. We are indebted to our colleague, Todd Hostager, for this insight.
7. We might add "data about strategy" to this list.
8. This union is the product of our rational reconstruction of the concept, and is one possible reconstruction that could be fashioned. See Chapter 1, note 18.
9. In order to ask this question, researchers must explicitly propose a context for application. The irony, of course, is that most strategy models violate our Principle about Persons yet purport to be tools for managers to apply!
10. These overlaps are quickly exhausted, however. See R. Edward Freeman, Daniel R. Gilbert, Jr., and Edwin Hartman, "Values and the Foundations of Strategic Management," *Journal of Business Ethics* (in press).
11. See Richard Rorty, "Texts and Lumps," *New Literary History*, 17, no. 1 (1985): 1–16.

12. One candidate for addition to this list is a Principle of Bargaining.

13. All this, of course, is predicated upon researchers and managers making the choice to see themselves making choices. The "choice to choose," as we have shown throughout this analysis, is obscured where the Principle about Persons is violated. This book suggests a different way to think about the issue of human agency, one that draws upon such arguments as those in Hazel E. Barnes, *An Existentialist Ethics*, Midway Reprint Edition (Chicago: University of Chicago Press, 1985).

INDEX

ABOUT THE AUTHORS

Daniel R. Gilbert, Jr., is an assistant professor of management at Bucknell University and a coauthor, with R. Edward Freeman, of *Corporate Strategy and the Search for Ethics*. Professor Gilbert received his B.A. from Dickinson College, M.B.A. from Lehigh University, and Ph.D. in business administration from the University of Minnesota. He has held staff and management positions with NCR Corporation and its subsidiary, NCR Comten.

Edwin Hartman is an assistant professor of management in the Faculty of Arts and Sciences, Rutgers University. Professor Hartman received his B.A. from Haverford College, B.A./M.A. from Balliol College at Oxford University, M.B.A. from The Wharton School at The University of Pennsylvania, and Ph.D. in ancient philosophy from Princeton University. He is the author of *Substance, Body, and Soul: Aristotelian Investigations* and *Conceptual Foundations of Organization Theory*. Formerly a consultant with Hay Associates, he has participated in a number of business ventures.

John J. Mauriel is an associate professor of business policy at the Carlson School of Management, University of Minnesota. He is also Director of the Bush Public School Executive Fellows and Bush Principals's Leadership Programs. Professor Mauriel received his A.B. from the University of Michigan and M.B.A. and D.B.A. degrees from the Harvard Business School. Author of more than twenty business school cases, he has served on numerous corporate boards of directors.

R. Edward Freeman is the Ellis and Signe Olsson Professor of Business Administration, and director of the Olsson Center for Applied Ethics at the Darden School, University of Virginia. He received his B.A. from Duke University and Ph.D. in philosophy from Washington University. In addition to the book with Professor Gilbert, Professor Freeman is author of *Strategic Management: A Stakeholder Approach*. He has consulted widely in the telecommunications industry.